Feeling Too Much

Highly Intuitive People, Setting Boundaries (Empath, Narcissists, Self-Aware, Intuition, Protect Yourself)

Kristine S. Everest

Feeling Too Much: Highly Intuitive People, Setting Boundaries (Empath, Narcissists, Self-Aware, Intuition, Protect Yourself)

Copyright © 2021 - All rights reserved. No part of this book may be reproduced in any form or by any means without permission in writing from the publisher, KSE Publishing. Please read the full disclaimer at the end of this book.

This book was self-published with the amazing help of Self-Publishing Made Easy Now! [1] . You can grab a free copy of the checklist that started my journey here: FREE Self-Publishing Checklist [2] .

[1]https://selfpublishingmadeeasynow.com/xpjv

[2]https://selfpublishingmadeeasynow.com/free_checklist

Table of Contents

Book 1 - Highly Intuitive People

The Ultimate Guide For Mastering Your Gift (Highly Sensitive, Empath, Life Changing, Survival Manual, Relationships)

1 - Introduction

Instinct

You live in a world that fuels your instinct. Numbers, theories, frameworks, and logic have very little place in your mind. That is the life of the highly intuitive.

Your past and upbringing have allowed you to nourish the other side of human capacity. You live on the other side of intellect. It's not the losing side, it's just the other side. It's the side that has kept us alive during the stone ages. It's the side that has allowed us to outlive the dinosaurs.

But what good is that side today; in a world that prizes intellect and gives laurels to the learned? What place is there for those that learn from their instinct? For those who trust their guts and their hearts more than their mind?

This is what this book is for. This book is here to tell you that your gift is not a curse. It is a rare blessing that will help you grow in an untold number of ways. You just need to awaken it and hone it to serve you.

This book will walk you through understanding and controlling your gift. It doesn't matter how long you've been living with your talents. Here, you will come to love what you have as it will help you get through life.

You may be in the dark about your talents or you may already be at peace with what makes you special; it doesn't matter. This book is designed to make you appreciate what you have and help you get the most out of your work, family, and other personal relationships. You won't just become more intuitive. You'll become an emotional beacon and stronghold for other people that do not share your talents.

2 - Understanding the Gift

It was the late Steve Jobs that tried to define the side of intuition. According to the founder of one of the biggest tech brands in the world, intuitiveness is a more natural form of human adaptability.

The iconic Carl Jung was one of those who attempted to label this capacity. According to him, people are divided into two sets. There are those who operate with logic and reason, questioning the environment, and using their knowledge to guide their decisions.

On the other hand, there are people like you; people with the gift. These are people with internal responses that come from instinct. Some experts would call it "thinking without thinking."

It's another facet of human intelligence that usually gets ignored in some of the more developed parts of the world. But in other areas such as India and other rural sections, intuitiveness has a greater importance than intellect. But what is intuitiveness? How is it different from other forms of intelligence?

Intuition Defined

The dictionary defines intuition as the capacity to understand a concept immediately, sans the logical reasoning.

In simpler terms, it's knowing something based on that gut feeling. You don't see any signs of danger, yet you know something bad is about to happen. You've barely known a person for five minutes but you know they're a good person. You've been in a room with someone for barely a minute and you already know something is bothering them.

These are examples of intuition. Don't be mistaken to think that it's an exclusive gift that only a select few people enjoy. It's a capacity everyone has. It's just that it's heightened and more developed in some more than others. Are you one of those people?

Intuition is not blind guesswork. It's something more than just claiming something and hoping it to be correct. It has a deeper and more profound connection with your senses and your feelings.

The funny part about intuition is that you yourself can't explain why you know these things. Has that ever happened to you? Just saying "I just feel it" when trying to explain your opinions to someone? That's just one of the many things that set intuitive people apart from the rest.

Telling If You Are Intuitive

What else sets you apart? What are those subtle differences you've noticed in you as you grew up and interacted with other people? According to experts, the highly intuitive do things differently and show signs of their gut prowess.

They Root Themselves in the Moment

The mind of the intuitive absorbs everything with their senses. The environment feeds their guts. They take note of what they see, hear, smell, and feel. Every little detail comes into their minds and creates a mental image that only they can see.

These sensations come together in their minds and help them act on rational impulses. Do you look around and take note of things? Are you tallying the general count of the people in the area? Do you immediately become aware of places with a lot of people? Can you immediately tell from which direction certain sounds are coming from?

As an intuitive individual, your gift requires you to gather information about your surroundings as soon as you put both feet on the ground. Your tendency to look around and observe comes as second nature. You're someone who "smells" danger even from a distance. You're also the last person to relax upon arrival at a new and unfamiliar place.

They Talk to Themselves

Highly intuitive people are not crazy; they just have an "inner voice" with which they have conversations. Some people call it a conscience. Others call it their guardian angel. Whatever name you have for it, you have a second-self inside of you, helping you process what you're feeling.

And no, the highly intuitive don't talk to themselves loudly while they converse with their impulses. They have silent discussions about their environments. They discern and determine what they're feeling at that certain moment.

Have you had many discussions with your inner voice? How many arguments have you had with yourself about how you feel and what you should do? You're no loner, but you value the time of self-reflection to enrich your impulsive nature.

In fact, you probably set aside a certain time of the day just to be alone with your thoughts. It could be while you prepare your breakfast. It could also be while you're in the shower. It may even be during your commute or drive to work and back home.

Those times are important to you. This is where you have those important discussions with yourself. That is your natural environment.

They Are Profound Thinkers

In line with talking to themselves, the highly intuitive can reach deep levels of thought because they always have someone on which to bounce their ideas. Your personal conversations with yourself don't just always end with close-ended thoughts.

You get deep into the why of the things you're feeling. At your very core, you don't just want to accept what you're feeling. You want to understand why you're feeling a certain way as well.

Do you always reroute your thoughts from your decisions all the way to a central principle you hold dear to yourself?

Have you always gone back to your core values every time you need to make a choice? Do you always double back from opportunities just to make sure your feelings and principles aren't compromised?

Because of this trait, intuitive people are the best people to approach when it comes to life decisions. This is because these people are beyond just weighing the pros and cons. For you, personal happiness, satisfaction, and even fulfillment become important factors to consider, further complicating discussions. This allows you to really get into someone's skin and find out what really makes someone happy.

They are Attuned with their Subconscious

Although the subconscious mind is beyond the grasp and understanding of many, the intuitive person cherishes the links they have between their waking minds and their automated consciousness.

Have you ever woken up from a dream and knew that it was your body trying to tell you something about yourself? As a highly intuitive individual, you understand that you have feelings and urges buried underneath your waking thoughts which only come to life when you sleep.

And when you're intuitive, you don't just have foggy visions when you dream. When you dream, you dream vividly. Details come with crystal clarity, allowing you to recall almost any detail the moment you wake up.

When this happens, you start to dig deep. Being the profound thinker that you are, you try to find meaning in these experiences and learn a little more about yourself with every dream you have.

They Never Bottle Their Feelings

For the intuitive, feelings aren't just excuses to cry or to act a certain way. Feelings are messages from our subconscious, trying to tell us what we deeply desire.

Those who are restrained by what other people think will try their best to hide their real feelings at the risk of being judged. You, on the other hand, openly embrace what you feel and enjoy a true openness with yourself.

Have you ever been stifled by a situation wherein you're expected to feel a certain way but you feel the opposite? You don't go with the stifling. You go against it and accept what you're feeling at that moment, recognizing it to be what's true.

They are Eternal Optimists

Since intuitive people are well-versed with what they feel and how to process these feelings, they're also better-equipped at dealing with setbacks and negative emotions.

You must have felt the same way at certain points in your life. You're not one to give in to wallowing but you're capable of accepting setbacks and loss. At the same time, you're also a firm believer of moving and welcoming new experiences to replace bad ones.

They Understand Purpose

Due to their love for profound thoughts, intuitive people appreciate the bigger picture in life. They know that their experiences lead to personal discoveries about themselves and that leads them towards a specific direction.

That is probably the reason you're reading this manual. Are you trying to find a purpose with your gift? What was it meant to do in your life? Where will this talent lead you? Better yet, where will you take your gifts once you know how to harness them?

They Are Sensitive to Others

Finally, their talents allow them to gain inklings if not glimpses of how other people around them are feeling. The highly intuitive are ideal empaths that can sense the general aura of an area and the people within.

Have you ever felt a change in mood without warning? Has the cold breath of negativity suddenly come over you despite your good temperament at that moment? You've probably picked up someone else's emotions.

Your observation of the environment and people lead you to ideas about how other people are behaving. Again, it's not guesswork. You feel it. You can sense their joy, hesitation, anger, and even sadness when you're with someone.

If you've come around these signs in your life, there's a big chance that you're highly intuitive. You pick up the subtleties that most people overlook in exchange for a different perspective.

3 - Types of Intuition

Just as there are different types of intellects, there are also different forms of intuition. They all manifest the same kind of knowledge, it's just that the method of delivery is different. Your gift may be prone to one kind more than another, but that doesn't mean it isn't useful.

Audio-Based Intuition

People who possess this type of intuition have deep and meaningful discussions within themselves. They've mastered this art so well that the voice inside their heads is very audible.

They use this voice as a guide which gives them their hunches in the form of straight messages.

- No
- Don't
- Go
- Yes
- Think

- Check

These are some examples of what they hear when their intuition kicks in. Their bodies and minds are wired to communicate with them using these short messages. These people claim they can really hear someone else speak to them, giving them advice on how to proceed.

Image-Based Intuition

If you have people who hear their hunches, there are also those who manifest their instinct in the form of images.

For this type, they can either dream of scenarios of suddenly conjure up a mental image of what they think might happen or what course of action they should take. It's a personal image for them that may or may not be symbolic in nature.

Sometimes, they still need to figure out the meaning of their images. Other times, they get specific answers. It all depends on how well they've honed their skills and how attuned they are with their bodies.

Sensation-Based Intuition

This is probably the most common form of intuition but certainly not the least useful. Here, intuitive people get their hunches from certain sensations that they experience. This is a broad approach which could have many possible outlets.

Their hunches could come in the form of butterflies in the stomach. It could also be a sudden wave of depression that comes over them for no reason at all. It may even be a sudden shot of pain through their temples.

These types of people use these sensations in relation to their situation. Immediately, they attribute what they're feeling to what is happening around them. Hence, they can zero in on their hunches.

Cognitive-Based Intuition

Finally, there are the types where their hunches set into their minds with ease. These kinds of intuitive people gain complete and specific thoughts. When they encounter someone, they can tell if these people are going through something or if they're about to do something drastic.

At the same time, their gift also gives them insight into what other people are feeling at that moment. Their hunches are a little more specific than other types, but this is the rarest of them all.

Usually, experts and psychics that have finely honed their skills are able to practice this form of intuition. Years and years of development and research will lead you to training your intuition to immediately give you full thoughts instead of feelings and images.

The Life of the Gifted

Yes, you have gifts that set you apart from others, but everything comes at a price. Being highly intuitive is not easy. Despite being special, you have myriad adjustments to make to yourself to adapt to the demands of the present day. That may not always be a walk in the park for you.

The Struggles of The Intuitive

Since you see the world differently, the way you interact with people is also different. One of the most difficult things you will experience as an intuitive person is explaining yourself to other people.

3 - TYPES OF INTUITION

How do you convince someone that you're right when all you're working on are your feelings and intuition?

In a world where logic is prized, you may find it hard to get your points and ideas across. This could cause misunderstandings with most people. This creates a need for you to widen your understanding and strengthen your patience with people who aren't ready to understand you on your level.

In turn, this skill becomes even harder to practice with people that want to take advantage of you. Given your natural talents, you can easily tell if people are telling you lies to win you over.

When this happens, it's difficult to remain civil and reciprocate their fake niceness. You know better than anyone the importance of honesty as you value it with yourself. How do you treat someone who isn't being honest with you at face value?

If you were to call someone out, what proof do you have? Intuitions are weak in terms of logic. How do you tell someone that they aren't being honest without offending them? How do you inform someone of their self-destructive behavior without ruining your relationship with them?

Because of these nuances, you may find it easier to keep your feelings and thoughts to yourself. This may cause you to shut yourself off from most people. In some cases, you could even be shutting out the people that care about you out of fear of misunderstanding.

This habit causes us to look inward most of the time with a pessimistic eye. We then become overly-sensitive of what we're thinking; to the point that we think it's wrong. In our quest for understanding, we end up misunderstanding our own talents and take our insights for granted.

Most intuitive people cling to a life of introversion. For them, meeting new people is an experience that requires energy.

Being social creatures, we still need human interaction. But for the introverted intuitive, it's more than just a meeting. For them, it's already a call to see if they can bond with someone on an emotional and intellectual level. That's why it costs them energy.

Unlike extroverts, introverts draw their energy from their

past experiences and their alone time. This is one of the reasons why it's important for talented individuals like yourself to partake in some form of meditation.

Introverts use this energy when they interact with other people. This is because they dig deep and share their thoughts with others. It's not because they've become attached, but because that's how they get to know someone else.

For them, small talk is a rudimentary waste of time. Some of the greatest intuitive people are self-confessed introverts. Look at J.K. Rowling, author of the iconic figure of Harry Potter and his myriad wizarding world that has charmed millions.

For her, small talk is boring and she considers herself inadequate for such things. She couldn't even speak to a stranger to borrow a pen.

You may have had similar experiences as well. Have you ever considered just keeping to yourself despite having a need that could be answered by reaching out to a stranger? Do social gatherings tire you out? Does the solace and privacy of your own space outshine even the largest of parties?

It's probably because you're intuitive.

In addition to that, we get lost in our own frustrations and end up belittling the things that we can do for ourselves and others. It's this large mix-up of feelings that could lead you down the wrong path of development. Hence, it's important to understand your gift and what makes it stand above the rest.

4 - The Advantages of The Highly Intuitive

Of course, if there are reasons to fear your gifts, there are also reasons to celebrate. Your talents aren't just for display. These are real-life advantages that give you benefits you cannot get anywhere else.

First off, you're better protected against those with malicious intent. This is because you can smell that from a mile away. You can see it in the way someone talks to you; and how they act towards your responses. You don't have to test them. You know they have ulterior motives.

This tells of untold advantages, to begin with. With your gift, you become an ideal judge of character. In business, that has untold benefits. You know who to trust and who to ignore. In relationships, you know where to invest your time and emotions. With friends, you get to filter who you should keep in your life.

Next, to that comes emotional intelligence. Take note, you're not emotional. You're emotionally intelligent. Those are two different things. One is a poorly-induced state of mind while the other is a hard-earned mental discipline.

This means you're aware of the presence of negativity in your life but at the same time, you're capable of letting these things influence you only up to a certain point.

With that, you move on faster. You get your life back earlier than most people. Don't misunderstand, though. As an intuitive person, you're not immune to the struggles of daily life. It's just that you're better equipped to handle these things compared to other people.

In addition to that, your capacity to deal with multitudes of emotions makes you an ideally-creative spirit. With all these feelings and ideas locked up inside, most intuitive people seek refuge in the release offered by the creative arts.

You could be entangled in music, the written word, film, acting and even painting! It doesn't matter what kind of art form you pursue. If it provides you with the creative expression you desire, you will embrace it with all your heart.

Another facet that your gifts give you is a firm resolution. The highly intuitive simply abhor standing on figurative sand.

As a person that takes everything into account, you can't

stand not thinking things through. You may be prone to overthinking but you're not one to be caught doing something you haven't thought about. For you, every decision is a firm one. When you commit to something, you give it your all because you've thought about it for countless times.

This makes you a great role model for others who can't seem to find their footing. Your commitment to your decisions is unlike any other, and this is all because you know how important it is to fully believe in something.

But what sets apart your gifts the most is your natural sensitivity to special life events. Because of your heightened emotions and control, you feel things on a deeper level than most people. The joy you feel is higher, as is your pleasure.

For you, a home-cooked meal isn't just a gastronomic trip. It's an act of love that fills your soul just as much as your belly. Experiences are very potent and important things for you.

And it's not just with food and get-togethers. Highly-intuitive people also enjoy more pleasure when it comes to sex. This is because making love doesn't just trigger physical cues for attachment. It also sets off emotional signals to create deep and lasting relationships.

5 - Survival Tips for the Gifted

On top of appreciating life and all its splendor, a big challenge poses itself on you every day. How will you make the right decisions with the right people and grow as an individual?

In a world where logic is valued in business and even in relationships, intuitive people may find it difficult to adjust to their environments and the people around them.

It's important for people like you to pick up on some tips to help improve the quality of your life.

Weed Out the Toxic People

First, determine who has what power over how you feel. Yes, the way you feel is something under your control, but there are people whose constant negativity and incurable misery will immediately seep into your good mood and turn things around.

These are known as toxic people. They infect you by giving off negative signals, feeding your intuition and poisoning your demeanor. You've probably met a few of these people already.

It could be that friend who always asks for advice for a miserable problem but does the exact opposite of what you say. It could be that in-law who is never happy with anything that you do. It could also be your romantic partner who has grown cold towards you.

Given your natural sensitivity, it's hard to ignore the influence of these people. If you work with them or live with them, their influence just grows in intensity. Take note of these people in your life.

When you've identified them, start avoiding them if you can't help them. Of course, the first thing you would want to do is to assist in improving their disposition in life, but if they've been miserable long enough, there's little even a gifted individual such as yourself can accomplish with them.

You don't need that kind of negativity in your life; especially in a life like yours. You could be enjoying such a lovely day with the best possible news you could ever receive but have it all taken away with one encounter with the wrong person. Your gifts could do that to you. Those people could do that to you.

You also want to save your energy and effort for the people

that matter. When you've labeled all the toxic people in your life, it leaves out the important people. These are the people who have proven themselves to be a positive influence in your life. And even if these people affect your negatively from time to time, they're the ones that deserve your attention.

Create a Habit of Thought-Watching

With your active imagination of complex thought processes, it's necessary for you to develop a habit of checking your train of thought. You may not like where your thoughts take you from time to time.

You could be in the middle of a stream of disappointment for a day which could then lead to chronic depression if you're not careful with the things that cross your mind.

On that same note, you could also be so happy that you're blinded from other issues that require your attention. You could get sometimes carried away by your thoughts that you miss the bigger picture, and intuitive individuals are all about the bigger picture.

When you notice yourself brooding over something, take a

step back and examine your thoughts. Ask yourself some probing questions to prove to yourself that what you're doing is not in your best interest.

- What am I thinking?
- Where will these thoughts take me?
- Am I brooding over this too much?
- Am I being melodramatic here?
- How will these thoughts help me get better?

Answering these questions will help you shift your focus towards a more positive goal and stop you from falling into emotional pits from which there is little escape.

On the same topic, it's also important to make an affirmation that you're changing your thoughts for the better. Claiming something within your mind can be a very powerful tool. Simply saying "This is not right. I will get better" to yourself is almost as good as doing it in real life; especially for someone like you. This is because mental messages to yourself are more powerful even than spoken words.

Practice Forgiveness

Just as the old saying goes, to err is human. To forgive, divine.

For the genuine intuitive person, slights and grudges are commonplace in our minds. You're the type who will never forget a good time had with friends. By that same virtue, you will also never forget a wrong that has been done to you.

It also gets deeper the more it hurts you. When you let your emotions get the best of you, you can't help but think about things more and more. You fill yourself with negative thoughts in an effort to console yourself when you're convinced that you're the victim.

When this happens, your behavior changes. You become mistrustful and distant, even from those that want to help you. This is because you've created a wall of hate that you've built so well with your developed emotions.

Naturally, you're the only one who can take down this wall; and it is done through forgiveness. And that is easier said than done.

A big weakness of intuitive people is that they have a hard time letting go of things that mean a lot to them. Whether it's bad or good, if it struck a nerve of strum a heartstring, you hold on to these things with such vigor.

And as you hold on to your anger and your desire to get even, you forget that you're also doing wrong to yourself. You're not letting yourself grow in your talents.

When you forgive, you don't just give other people the chance to move on. You give yourself the amazing opportunity to learn from your experiences and be an example to other people.

You get stuck on ideas of hatred because you no longer see the benefits of forgiving people. The central idea in your head in anger is getting even. You want to see justice meted out. You want to see karma in action. You believe that when it happens, you will be satisfied.

This couldn't be further from the truth. Even if karma came around the corner and tit-for-tat is complete, you're still just going to be as miserable as ever. It get even worse over time because the longer to persist on an idea, the more likely it is to become a truth with you.

Have a "Safe Space"

If meditation and clearing your thoughts are important to the mind, then you should have a designated place for meditation at home.

It doesn't have to be a full room with electronics and speakers and diffusers. It's an ideal place, but not necessary. All you need is a small corner wherein you can affirm no negative thoughts will enter.

Some people will call it their happy place. Some call it their quiet corner. It doesn't matter what name you call it. What matters is that nothing negative should enter that space, because that is where you hone your thoughts and realign your focus.

When you step into that space, you should be prepared for meditation and relaxation.

It can be next to your bed or a corner of your bed. It could also be a small corner of your room. It can also be right underneath your shower head. This place should hold a very special place in your heart and it doesn't have to make sense to other people. In fact, you shouldn't let other people with negative thoughts into that space if they aren't meditating with you.

Maintain a Feeling of Gratitude

This works wonders even for those who aren't "gifted". Many successful people from likes of Einstein, Warren Buffet, Charlie Munger, J.K. Rowling and even Steve Jobs emphasize how important it is to be thankful.

And it's not just being thankful to your god. It's also being thankful to the people that have helped you get the things that you need and want.

When you're thankful, there's no room for resentment, anger, jealousy, and pride. You are humbled just to the right level. In such a state, much can be achieved.

You work harder. You enjoy working hard to show respect to your benefactors. You eliminate competition from your mind. You're clear of malice and your focus is unshakable under the premise of personal shame.

Which is why it's a good idea to think of things for which you're thankful before starting your day. It sets the mood of the day and empowers you to take on whatever challenges that lie ahead of you.

Love Your Gift Like a Child Loves a Toy

Yes, you're special. Yes, you can do, see, feel, and experience things that many people cannot. Despite that, it doesn't mean that you are part of an elite group of people that segregate themselves from society. In more interesting cases, intuitive people such as yourself are the ones that are segregated negatively because of your unique insights.

Your talents are not for show only. They are meant to enrich your life and the lives of those around you. Your gifts aren't meant to make other people jealous. They are meant to make other people stronger.

With that thought in mind, don't treat your talents like a prized stallion that you spoil daily with ridiculous customs and rules. It won't grow that way.

Instead, love your gift the way a child loves their toys. They play with them lovingly, enjoying every second of entertainment and joy they get. They devote their time and attention to shaping their imaginations with their toys, creating small worlds that only they know about.

On the same note, they will take their toys to the mud, to the dirt and even to the streets if they could. You should do the same with your gifts. They should be with you and used whenever you can.

6 - Honing the Gift

Just like any other talent, your intuition fades into obscurity when it is not practiced. Yes, it will always be there, dormant at times, but it would be a shame not to develop your skills and live life to the fullest.

Interestingly, how do you develop something that doesn't follow a rational or logical process? Traditional methods may not be suitable for such a gift. What you need are modern-day approaches.

Mindfulness Meditation

As simple as this sounds, this may well be one of the most difficult forms of meditation to master. This is not because of religious or spiritual ties. In fact, mindfulness has nothing to do with these concepts.

At its very core, mindfulness is the capacity to channel your focus on the moment. This is something almost anyone can achieve with the proper guidance. You don't need to follow a specific philosophy or preach a certain faith. All you need to do is to live in your present state.

That may be easier said than done. Whether we admit it or

not, we are all residents of our own thoughts. These thoughts could sometimes hinder us from living in the moment.

This is especially true today. We live in a world full of issues and challenges that cloud our minds and keep us locked in our desires. I want this. I want that. When will it happen? It's easy to become lost in a self-destructive dialogue with yourself.

Interestingly, quieting this inner dialogue will help sharpen your intuition. Yes, it was mentioned that the intuitive are great with their inner dialogue. Despite that, your inner voice could lead you astray as you try to figure out things.

Mindfulness meditation will help you realign your sights and clean your mental slate. Fortunately, it doesn't take years to master. In fact, you can do it right now.

Before putting down this book to practice, read these instructions carefully. Find a place in which to meditate. It doesn't have to be a spiritual area in which meditation is usually done. This doesn't even have to be at a church or a temple.

Finding a quiet corner of the room with a comfortable chair will suffice. When looking for a spot, it's important that there should be as little audible and visual distractions as possible. Meditating in a busy and hectic area can be difficult.

Once you've found a place in which to meditate, place yourself in a comfortable position. The good thing about this is that you can choose to either lean back into a reclining chair or to completely lie down. The choice is up to your preferences.

In a comfortable position, you can now begin a short mindfulness meditation sequence. This shouldn't take more than five minutes to complete.

Begin the sequence by closing your eyes. Mindfulness meditation is a process wherein you empty your thoughts and absorb your environment. This means the first thing you should do is to recognize the thoughts you're harboring at that moment and let it go.

As soon as you close your eyes, try to paint yourself a mental image of your breath. This task alone should help you clear your thoughts. Try to imagine your lungs expand and decompress with each breath you take.

Remember to keep your eyes closed as you breathe. To make things more vivid, picture your breath as it enters your body, finding its way into your lungs and mixing with your blood. Feel yourself become refreshed with every breath.

At the same time, also take note that your head feels lighter with every breath you take. Don't worry if your body moves around a lot as you breathe in and breathe out. That's part of the experience.

Don't even worry about the method of breathing that you're using. As long as it's comfortable, keep whatever pace you want. What's important is that you're paying attention to only your breathing.

After a few breaths, you will notice that you cannot stop yourself from not breathing. This is a sign that tells you your body has shifted breathing from a subconscious activity to a conscious one. You now should tell yourself to breathe. Don't be alarmed by this. It's a sign that means your meditation is going as planned.

As you begin to relax, you will also find that your thoughts may start drifting. You may start going back to whatever it is you were thinking before meditating. This is also a natural error that a lot of beginners make.

When this happens, take another deep breath and realign your focus towards your breathing. The purpose of this activity is to help you clear your mind, not help you think about something else.

As you feel your head getting lighter from the breathing, ease into your position and continue visualizing your breath as it nourishes you. As you get more relaxed, you're telling your body to stop implementing its stress responses and that you're safe.

You'll now you're done meditating when you've realized that you're no longer stressed and have a more positive demeanor at the end of the activity. At this point, don't just open your eyes and abruptly end the meditation, that's one way to waste all that time you've spent meditating.

Instead, take one last breath and slowly open your eyes as you exhale. You will notice that your perspective of your environment has changed a bit and things seem a little brighter. That is how mindfulness works.

Other Forms

You'll be pleased to know that this short activity is just one of many mindfulness exercises that you can do on your own. The one you just finished is known as mindfulness breathing.

Other ways you can practice mindfulness also include body inspections. Instead of focusing on your breathing, you turn your focus towards what the various parts of your body are feeling.

This is done by making mental notes of the sensations that your skin encounters. What are your hands feeling? How does the fabric of your clothes feel against your skin? What sensations are your feet feeling while they're inside your shoes? Answering these questions as you meditate can help shift your focus and clear your mind.

These are known as body checks. More advanced users put together combinations of body checks and breathing meditations to get the most out of their quiet time. The longer you practice your mindfulness, the easier it will become for you to achieve harmony with your inner voice.

7 - Journal Maintenance

You may be hesitant about the apparent worth of a journal to an intuitive person, but nothing could be more enriching than a written collection of your personal thoughts.

Most people consider the act of keeping a journal a tiresome one. For the talented intuitive person, a journal is a log-book of the soul. With a journal, you get to give you inner voice a physical form.

This method of honing your talents doesn't follow the same route as conventional journal-writing. For the intuitive, journal keeping is a chance to let your mind free and wreak havoc on a clean sheet of paper.

Primarily, you don't really need a fancy journal or a diary to begin. You just need a notebook on which you can write. From there, the magic begins.

Before diving in, be sure to mark the date and time of your writing. It really helps you piece your thoughts together when you are more specific with your time.

As you begin your entry, try not to pay too much attention to a central theme and motif. The purpose of a journal is to let your thoughts run wild, not to create a preconceived idea. That will only frustrate you as you write.

When starting, don't worry about the first few words that come out. They're usually what gets the ball rolling. You can start with almost anything. Try asking yourself a question and see where your inner dialogue takes you.

Don't get frustrated if your work isn't something appealing to the immediate reader. Your writing there isn't meant for the eyes of other people. It's more of a tool you can use to reflect patterns in your thinking. It helps you see if you've been circling around a repeating concept or idea. It will also tell you if you're going through chronic stress over time.

Another interesting facet of journal-keeping is that you can also use it as a dream-log. Other people call it a dream-journal but the concept remains the same. Besides setting aside a good hour every day to scribble your inner conversations, you can also use a journal to capture your dreams before you forget them throughout the day.

8 - Indulging The Other Senses

Many experts refer to your intuition as the "sixth sense" which encompasses knowledge gained from all our 5 sense organs. Interestingly, developing these rudimentary senses is a great way to develop your intuition.

You may not notice it fully, but feedback from your senses fuels your instinct. This works similarly to the way animals detect danger in their environment. Take note that they don't just use their eyes to gauge threats. Some animals are even sensitive to precipitation in the air to watch out for storms.

This then leads to a unique question. How do you pay attention and sharpen your senses?

Using principles from mindfulness meditation, honing your senses requires you to ground yourself in a moment to assess the sensations around you. Placing yourself in experiences with diverse sensory stimuli will help promote such growth.

Pay attention to your senses as you experience things. Sitting back on a massage chair is certainly a comfortable experience. In that chair, try to determine which body parts of yours are getting attention from the chair. What sort of alleviation are you feeling? Is it releasing tension? Is it relaxing your muscles?

Do the same thing with a good meal. Does it just taste good? Try to segregate the flavors you're experiencing. Are you detecting hints of your favorite ingredients? What elements of your meal do you find most striking in your dish? How well do the dishes complement each other on your palette?

On the same note, sharpen your sense of smell by exposing yourself to various aromas. Aromatherapy is an ideal way to de-stress and sample the fragrant scents of various flowers and plants. Acquainting yourself with these scents will broaden your sensory vocabulary and leave you refreshed at the same time.

Take this process to every sensory experience you have. The best thing about this is that you're always going through sensations. It's just a matter of finding the right moments to practice.

One of the best ways to bombard your senses is to go hiking. You don't necessarily have to climb a mountain to experience something good. Sometimes, a good walk at the park will suffice. Being one with nature allows you to hone these senses, just as Mother Nature intended for us.

Note Your Body Signals

Different people have different descriptions of a "gut feeling". For some, their innards twist up and they get restless when something is about to go wrong. For others, butterflies in their stomach start to form in anticipation for something.

How does your body communicate with you? What sort of signals does it give? This is where keeping a journal comes in very handy. As you age and mature, your body develops different kinds of telling signals to alert you of your intuition. Writing them down will give you a better guide to understanding yourself.

The only way for you to get opportunities to read your body is when you're forced to rely on your intuition. Go on an adventure. Better yet, plan an adventure. Even if you haven't left yet, the experience of putting together a trip makes you feel all sorts of emotions as you make decisions.

As you plan, take note of how your intuition communicates.

Do you twist up when you think about certain places? Do you get queasy as you consider visiting some in-laws out of state? Do you feel relaxed as you target going to the hometown of a childhood friend? Take note of these things as you plan and as you travel.

Additionally, the break from routine will help liven up your senses. Nothing is better at dulling a sharp knife than repeated use. Breaking away from the drudgery of everyday life is a good way to immerse yourself in experiences that will sharpen your instinct.

Unleash Your Creativity

One of the biggest reasons why intuitive people are creative is because they appreciate their artistic outlets. Who better to enjoy the creative release of creation that someone that embodies the very notion of creativity?

Being an intuitive person, you are a breeding ground for ideas. Simple concepts turn into complex patterns for you, waiting to be expressed. When something hits you, it comes just as suddenly as one of your hunches. They are unplanned, therefore, meaningful.

Your stories, experiences, and emotions make for great creative material. Even if you're currently bereft of inspiration, your intuition floods you with possibilities. You just need to be open enough to see them as they come to you.

The best part about this is that the more you express yourself, the more attuned you become to your creative tendencies. The better you understand your emotion. You go deeper into yourself, learning more as you reach the apex of your creativity.

Never Force It

There are times when you literally need your intuition to step in and it doesn't come to you. It could as you sit in front of that job offer. It could also be when you're talking to that person who's trying to borrow money from you.

When your instincts don't kick it, it can be frustrating; like never being able to find a pen when you need one. When this happens, you prod yourself, blaming your inadequacy. This is no way to hone your talents.

According to psychics and other experts, intuition is more likely to take place when you're calm and relaxed. Remember that this talent springs from a deep and satisfying relationship between your waking mind and your subconscious.

With that being said, it is necessary to recognize your stress signals and to work on clearing your mind so that your instincts kick in with more efficiency. On top of that, you get clearer messages and hunches in a relaxed state rather than an agitated one.

Appreciate the benefits of approaching every situation with a calm mind. It's a concept that works well for both the logical mind as well as the intuitive one. Reasoning and feeling work better when you're not clouded by thoughts of frustration and confusion.

On the other hand, it's important to also recognize the difference between apathy and calmness. Your gifts don't require you to lose concern in order for them to work. They require you to understand the value and weight of your situation and to look at things through a disciplined perspective. You don't need razor-sharp focus to work your intuition; just a relaxed state of mind.

Testing Your Intuition

What other way is there to practice a skill than to use it in real life situations?

Putting your intuition into practical use may be easier than you think. Take the news, for instance. It is full of people, events, and emotions for you to read. You just have to use a different eye when watching.

Take a certain politician, for example. Let's say that this politician is involved in a big controversy that affects his public standing. Being a public figure, this person needs to make a statement or take a certain course of action.

Tap into your intuition and try to get a feel of what this person might too. It's not plain guesswork if that's what you're thinking. It's more of hypothesis-creation.

Look at this person and try to see what they're feeling. Shame and frustration could be good places to start. Try to dig deeper and see how they work. You also have access to this person's history, with them being a politician.

Take those things into account and say what you would do if

you were in their position. Would you come clean? Would you deny? Would you blame someone else? Would you step down from office? Would you just disappear? There are so many options available. And using your gift, your guess will probably be just as close as what will happen in real life.

Even if that isn't the case, you can still learn from your mistakes. Compare what you've thought of to what really happens. From there, you can see what points you might have overlooked. From that point, it's just a matter of adjusting your thought process to make more accurate readings.

If you're not a fan of the news, you can also practice on the people around you. Be with other people, even if you're not talking to them. Observe them as they go about their daily routine. Are you noticing changes in their behavior? Are they exhibiting something out of the ordinary? You may want to talk to them and learn more. You'll be surprised at what you can learn.

It is through these activities that you can better acquaint yourself with your gift. The more you use it, the better and sharper it gets. With enough practice, you'll be able to see things from a mile away.

9 - Intuition Vs Naivete

Whether you're a beginner with your talents or a veteran with your gifts, you will have come across the notion that your intuition could be nothing more than your own vanity.

One of the biggest challenges faced by any intuitive person is to see the value in their own gifts and look beyond what other people say about them. And mind you, people will say a lot of things.

- "You're lucky."
- "You cheated."
- "You're talking to someone on the inside."

When other people doubt your intuition, there's a good chance you'll start doubting it as well. It's easy to ask for logic from something that doesn't need logic to operate in the first place. And when someone asks you to explain how you know these things, you tend to lose credibility when you say "I just know these things."

Trusting Yourself

This is the first thing you need to do. Accept the fact that your gut feeling is trying to tell you something and that it doesn't want to lead you astray. Yes, you're in control of your own body. Your senses, instinct, and heart know that all too well. Have you ever seen a person that intuitively wants to lead themselves into terrible decisions?

What other people say about your intuition is irrelevant to how effective it is. You're the only person you have to convince. If you can't even do that at, then your gift becomes a curse, right down to its core.

To gain more confidence in your gut feeling, some retrospection is required. Look back at some good life decisions you've made. Don't forget to be thankful for what those decisions have brought you. Using your vivid imagination and memory, try to remember what you were feeling when you made those decisions.

What was your instinct telling you? Go back to that time and verify if your intuition served you well. Most likely, you will find that your gut was telling you it was good as well. You'll be surprised to know how accurate your instinct can be.

You may also be wondering about bad decisions in your life.

Did you also follow your intuition during those times? Did you gut and instinct lead you astray? You may be inclined to blame your intuition for getting you into trouble as well, but that's only because you're missing on things.

During the times that you made poor decisions, were you only relying on your intuition? Take a closer look. Did you also let the opinions of other people affect your judgment? Were there other factors involved?

How about your other feelings? Were you hungry, sad or desperate when you made these decisions?

Sometimes, because of doubt, we try to find logical reasons to support our intuitions. This may or may not be the best idea. Finding a logical reason to back up a decision your instinct tells you to be right may not be the best idea at times.

Don't try to back up your gut feeling with more reasons. There will be times that those two won't mix and you'll end up twice as confused. This will dilute your resolution and lead you to half-baked solutions that won't do you any good.

10 - Understanding The Confusion

Where do you draw the line between intuitive thinking and hoping for the best? Fortunately, these two things share one core focus; the outcome.

How do you view the outcome of a certain situation? Here is where you get to test your intuition. Do you feel something will happen? Or do you want something to happen?

Sometimes, you could be blinded by your needs that we misunderstand what your intuition is telling you. You could really be hurting for the money, which is why you might tend to think that a shady business deal looks like a lifesaver. You could be lonely and depressed, which could lead you to think a friendship with a certain character could be beneficial for you.

When this happens, we tend to ignore what our gut is telling us. In turn, we mistake these needs as our intuition speaking to us, telling us to preserve ourselves and jump into something that may not be good for us.

When things go sour, we end up blaming our "poor" instincts and wish we knew better. If this has ever happened to you, it has to change now lest you repeat those mistakes despite having earnest and pure intentions.

Harboring A Desire

This central notion is what separates intuition and wishful thinking. Although desiring something in life is an inherently good thing, channeling all our focus and determination on this specific desire may not help us achieve this outcome.

Take, for instance, a cheating ex for whom you still have affection. Should this person ask for another shot at a relationship with you, what will your intuition say?

Naturally, the history of cheating will be a prevalent factor. There is proof of infidelity. This will certainly cause your intuition to tell you that getting back together is a bad idea.

However, your affection and desire to be happy with this person interfere with your better judgment. Although this is a classic contrast between the mind and the heart, the presence of a harbored desire makes things more complicated.

It's not conceited if you're wondering. Humans are just built that way. A life without a longing for something is not a life lived at all. What's important is that we use this desire to create purpose in our lives, and not let our yearnings cloud our judgment.

Separating Knowing From Wanting

It's unwise to purge yourself of desires that could cloud your judgment. Even the most dedicated monks need further clarity in their beliefs. You would be a completely different person without desires of any nature.

This is where your true empathic nature will arise. Being able to tell apart your desires and your hunches are the mark of a true intuitive. To do that, you need the firm habit of retrospection.

This is simply the habit of taking a step back and examining yourself through an emotional perspective. Here, you ask yourself a series of questions that will help you unearth the true nature of your feelings.

- Do I feel good about this because I want it?
- Am I jumping into this too quickly?

You can ask yourself any question to get to the heart of the issue. What's important is that you're aware of what you want and what your body is telling you. It's good if they're the same thing but never overlook the possibility that they might be very different.

As an intuitive, you probably already have this habit. The trick here is to place a goal at the start of your retrospection. Don't just verify what you're feeling. Try to segregate your desires from your intuition so that you can commit to something with all your heart.

The Fear of Vulnerability

On a fundamental level, your intuition serves a specific purpose; to save yourself. Along with the many other abilities that come with this talent, your instinct is designed to deter you from harming yourself.

On that same level, it can be said that it follows the natural state of humans to avoid pain. It's part of what makes us human. It's what makes us mortal. We value this mortality and ensure that we don't shorten our existence by our own accord.

As an intuitively gifted individual, this desire to stay safe becomes magnified, just like any other feeling you possess. You feel it a little more than everyone else. This also means you cherish it on a higher level as well.

With that said, your appreciation of a safe and comfortable environment immediately shows in your mood. At the same time, when something threatens your safety and well-being, you're one of the first people to show that fear.

It is that vulnerability that can hinder you from reaching your full potential as an intuitive. This is one of the first things you have to overcome in order to hone your instinct.

Accepting Vulnerability

What pushes us away from our weaknesses the most is the prospect of them damaging us in ways we clearly imagine. On that note, an intuitive does more than just imagine their vulnerabilities getting the best of them. They feel what it's like; and its unbearable for them.

Because of their sensitivities, intuitive people are more prone to shying away from exposing their weaknesses. They guard it with their very lives, only permitting a select few to get to know them well.

With all that being said, you'll be surprised to know that you can still find strength in being vulnerable. It just takes a different perspective.

According to psychology experts, we humans are predisposed to hate showing weakness. It's just not in our nature. It makes us seem untrustworthy and unlovable. These are the last two things anyone would want for themselves.

But then again, what do you have to lose when you let other people know that you need them? What exactly happens to someone when they reveal their vulnerabilities? What comes after the terrifying thought of someone letting you down and leaving you to your fears?

This is what most people fail to see. We can be so shrouded in our fears that we no longer see what we stand to gain when we let other people in and show them that we need them.

We win lasting relationships. We win the kind of people we want in our lives; people that understand and accept us and our gifts. We get people who are just as willing to adjust to our needs as we are capable to adjust to theirs.

On that same note, we also filter out the people we don't need. We get to see who can be there for us and who can't. What's after that is a strong network you trust. What you get is a circle of meaningful relationships that will help you grow as a person. That is worth the fear.

No, that won't be easy by any means. After all, you have to break a few eggs to make an omelet. Yes, it will hurt. Yes, you will be let down. Not everyone you let in will be worth the trouble, but that's where your intuition comes in.

Be careful of the people you let in, but don't shut everyone out for fear of getting hurt. It's alright to be scared, but it's never fine to live in constant fear. Yes, our fear is natural and born from our struggles and past failures. But with that said, it is our lasting relationships and bonds that make us human.

How To Overcome Fear

It's not enough just to be careful. Do you even have the strength and will to start? One thing about highly intuitive people is that they set up a barrier around themselves that no one else sees.

When you live in that barrier long enough, you tend to forget how to take it down when the right people come around. You become so enveloped in lonely comfort that you would rather live with what you have than enrich your life in the company of other people. That's one thing that makes it difficult to understand you.

To your surprise, it doesn't take an extraordinary individual to break down those walls. As much as you're yearning for relationships that breach your barriers, it is you that has to take them down. That is easier said than done.

The first thing you need to do is to stop overthinking.

Highly intuitive people can be very imaginative. For them, a simple meeting isn't just a pleasant experience. It's a sign of many great adventures with someone. It's a collection of happy memories waiting to be made.

You're not melodramatic, though. You just like thinking ahead to all the good times you'll be having with someone. That doesn't just apply to romantic relationships. You do the same thing with potential friendships.

When you start peering into the future, you start creating

these mental images of what you want to happen with your bonds and where you want to take them. You suddenly make plans in your head and jump into conclusions.

Stop for a while and have yourself a reality check. Here, mindfulness meditation works wonders. When you start getting carried away by your instinct and imagination, take a breather and root yourself in the moment.

When you fail to stop yourself from thinking too far ahead, you end up making unrealistic expectations for these people which is a sure-fire way to become disappointed and miserable.

No, you're not controlling and manipulative. You're just hopeful and positive. That can be a good thing but only up to a certain extent. Keep your feet rooted and simply enjoy what you have at the moment. There will be a time for you to think of future adventures.

The next thing you need to learn is empathy.

Yes, you have needs in a relationship and bond with someone. Sure, you have requirements that certain people seem to meet at the moment. Despite that, you're not the only one who could badly need a meaningful connection.

Before you find the courage to let someone in, you need to learn what it means to be let in as well. Don't be clouded by your own needs that you fail to see how your presence is important to other people as well.

Don't forget that your needs come with a set of talents and sensitivities that make you a great companion and friend for other people. Use your gifts to create meaningful relationships with other people that need it.

When you experience what it's like being there for someone, you'll better appreciate what it's like when someone is there for you. You'll value this bravery more than ever, making you look over your fear of being vulnerable.

The last thing you have to learn is to communicate your need.

It doesn't come as simply saying "I need you in my life."

It usually doesn't even have to be a short and powerful statement that grabs the spotlight. Asking someone to be there for you doesn't have to be such a dramatic event. You can get your message across to the right people with a series of meaningful statements that hit the right spots.

- "Thank you for the time. I really needed that talk."
- "Thanks for seeing me today. I could really use a friend."
- "Your encouragement really helped me today."
- "I am very entertained by our discussions."
- "I look forward to our meetings and exchanges every time."

As you can see from these statements, one sentiment stands out the most; gratitude.

Be thankful for the people that enrich your life. They are there for a reason. One thing people are so good at doing is overlooking the small things and over-dramatizing the big things.

Very few people understand the power of gratitude. When we are thankful for something, we rid ourselves of any fear or negative intention within ourselves. It's like cleaning our slates and realigning our focus towards more positive ventures.

When we are thankful, we attract better things towards ourselves. When other people see that, they become more comfortable around us and in turn, become part of our lives.

Being thankful is one way to attract the right people into your life. Never think about what one relationship means for you. Instead, think of what your relationship with this person could mean for them.

You may be intuitive, but you'll never know what it's like to be someone else once you've walked in their shoes. You may gain glimpses of their personal struggles and affairs, but the only way you'll get more depth is when someone lets you in.

You don't have to be direct with what you need. Simply be thankful and others will see that you cherish whatever bond you have with them. Once you've done that, you're bringing yourself closer to the right people without even realizing it. Sooner or later, your fear of becoming vulnerable with someone fades away and drowns in a sea of trust and positivity.

11 - A Life of Compassion and Wanting the Best

One very big part of being intuitive is the need to make the right decisions. The word “right” itself has a very deep meaning for you. It’s the first thing you yearn when you get your inklings.

Because of the way you handle your emotions, it’s natural for you to want what’s best for everyone concerned. It’s not a matter of principle. It’s a matter of your talents.

Because you can sense what others could be feeling at a given moment, you take it upon yourself to make sure everyone is happy. This natural compassion may take you to great heights, and may also cause you great frustration.

Wanting What’s Right

Despite your ability to notice if something’s wrong, you can easily get stuck pondering on what would be beneficial for everyone. An interesting facet of an intuitive individual is that they are inherently compassionate and sharp at the same time.

You’re well-designed to detect deception but your heart is

that of a humanitarian. This interesting contrast makes up most of your life struggles as an intuitive.

Finding the right mix between righteous and merciful can be a daunting task for the gifted intuitive. Sometimes, it even gets to the point wherein you take on the problems of other people as your own because you can feel their pain on a certain level.

This is where you have to learn how to pick your battles. It starts with accepting a single notion:

Your happiness and contentment will not come from solving everyone's problems. At times, what is best for everyone may not include your needs. So you end up sacrificing on your end just to please everyone but you end up with the short end of the stick. This leaves you defeated.

But you can't help it. You know the satisfaction of doing the right thing more than anyone else because of your gift.

You can't please everyone, even if you think you're doing what's right for everyone. Sure, your intuition tells you what is right, but that may not be the same idea shared by the people you're trying to help.

You have a deeper understanding compared to other people. It's best not to expect people to see things the way you do. The sooner you realize and accept this universal truth, the lighter you'll feel when you walk away from events that are out of your control. Sometimes, the right thing to do is to mind your own business.

But you have to want it to make it worthwhile. As an intuitive individual, you detest the notion of giving up on something, especially when you've dedicated yourself. You have to draw the line between doing what's right for everyone and preserving your own happiness. You're special, alright; but you're not a superhero.

It is when you see the emotional plight of other people that you forget to treasure your own balance. When that happens, you dive deep into someone else's affairs with the intent of helping them.

Before doing that, take a step back and do some retrospection and self-assessment. Learn to love yourself a little when you feel the need to take on someone else's problems.

12 - Understanding Bodily Cues

In line with living with your gift, it's important to be attuned to the way your body operates. Regardless of the type of intuition you receive, it is important to recognize the signs your body gives you when it is trying to tell you something.

Even if your intuition works by giving you images, your body will still try to give you hints about a certain situation. Take note that your intuition is not rooted in your conscious mind. It dances in your subconscious. It happens even if you don't tell your body; just like breathing.

On that same train of thought, take a good look at yourself in certain situations. You can also go back to specific events in your life and review the way you behaved and how your body interacted with you.

Do you notice certain habits that come out of you in certain situations? What were the nature of those events? What sensations flooded you during those times? As you answer these questions, write them down in your journal to keep track of your progress.

Positive Signs

Start with the good events in your life. They don't have to be big, important undertakings such as weddings and work promotions. Your intuitive body also sends signals during the simplest joys in life; such as a short afternoon chat with a friend over coffee.

Although different intuitive individuals have different ways their bodies communicate with them, experts point out to a few commonalities that stand out during positive events.

Primarily, your shoulders tend to relax during good times as an indicator that everything is going smoothly. They aren't tensed and raised in anticipation of a threat.

If you're with someone with whom you're comfortable, you also tend to lean towards their direction. When you're enjoying a good conversation, which seems to be going in interesting directions, your body shows its interest as well by optimizing your position to hear well and understand more efficiently.

Another thing to note is that your breathing tempo is normalized. You're not hyperventilating from stress because your body isn't intercepting any potential threat to you.

You will note that breathing can be either a conscious or unconscious effort. When your body delegates breathing to your subconscious, it becomes a great indicator of your current state.

Finally, one of the biggest signs of positive times ahead is the presence of goosebumps. This happens when you're anxious about something good or influential. You may have experienced these at the onset of something really good or right in the middle of something nice as it happens.

When your body intuitively does these things, it's time to relax further in the knowledge that everything is going to be alright.

Negative Signs

If your body communicates to you in the presence of good times, then it also has warning signs that tell you something is amiss. Experts have also found some common behaviors our bodies use to tell us to double back and reexamine our situations.

First, if breathing is normalized during good times because of your subconscious comfort, it then becomes restricted and hampered when your body is perceiving a threat to your well-being.

Interestingly, you hold your breath unknowingly at certain points as if to brace yourself for something shocking or unwelcome. This can also be accompanied by a tightening of the throat which makes breathing a more difficult task.

Another sign is the iconic chill down the spine. It may or may not be a cold wind going down your back, but your spine shivers from a rush of hormones coming from your central nervous system.

On top of that, you can also feel discomfort in your stomach. These aren't the butterflies you expect during romantic affairs, but a sinking and twisting feeling urging you to go to the bathroom and reexamine yourself.

Along with those, your body could also alert you to old wounds and other ailments you may have. You could have a sudden headache or an old scab would start twitching.

When your body uses pain to get your attention, it's usually because you're subconsciously anticipating a worst-case scenario and your action is required immediately.

These are just a few ways your body speaks to you. The more you listen, the better message you'll get from your intuition. Hence, it is important to keep a journal so that you can log your various states throughout the day. This is the only way you can effectively learn how your body tells you things.

Stress For The Highly Intuitive

Besides signals, your body also responds to stress differently from other people. What may stress others may not be so bothersome to you. On that same note, what could be dauntingly stressful for you may not seem like a big issue for other people.

This is why you should be aware of what triggers your stress reactions. For a gifted intuitive such as yourself, you're probably to incur stress from a certain number of things.

One of the foremost triggers of your stress is the need to do what's right all the time. This may be an easy choice at times, but when it requires a little more digging and some trial and error, it becomes frustrating.

This is especially true when you have multiple decisions to make at the same time. This could happen when you're planning a vacation with your friends or deciding what movie to see with some of your relatives.

In another sense, you're also a perfectionist. Because of your sensitivity to yourself, you know what it feels when you don't give 100% of yourself to a certain task. When you can't consider your work to be perfect, it gets to you. You then question your capabilities regardless of what other people are saying.

Another thing that triggers your stress reactions is your propensity to overthink.

Being highly intuitive, you can't help but learn new things about yourself. You give great priority to experiences that teach you knew things about yourself and the people around you.

In turn, you begin to worry about almost everything you do, no matter how mundane the task is. This is because the mind of an intuitive individual is a very active one. It may be full of impulsive thoughts and sentiments, but that doesn't mean it's not at work. You just don't see the ticking clocks and gears inside your head but they're there, spinning around like there's no tomorrow.

And this could cause a lot of worry for you. Combined with your tendency to be perfect, you could end up constantly questioning the purpose of the things you do and the manner in which you're doing them.

This puts you in a state of constant self-checking. Without proper de-stressing methods, you could end up suffering from chronic stress even without the interference of other people.

To counteract this, experts suggest the implementation of meaningful rituals throughout the day to help you appease the internal cynic within.

One of these rituals is to meditate in the morning. It doesn't have to a religious experience. It just has to be a unifying one that sets all your worries aside and shifts your energy from tense to relaxed.

Try setting aside at least fifteen minutes in the morning to meditate and clear your thoughts. One of the best things you can do at this time is some mindfulness meditation.

This is especially helpful when your day doesn't start out the way you wanted. When you wake up to demands and complaints and other concerns, you know things are going to get rough.

They get rougher when your mind and body aren't prepared to meet the challenges of the day. This short morning ritual will help you get your head in the game and help you maintain your focus.

Eating Right

It's only natural that the food you eat also affects the way your body communicates with you. Your food choices shouldn't just revolve around the notion of being physically fit. Your diet has to also help keep your intuition sharp.

After years of study, psychics and healing gurus have determined that your intuition and instinct rely on your endocrine glands to alert your body and keep your senses sharp. This is why you should make it a point to ingest food items that will promote the growth and proper maintenance of these glands.

For that, your first choice should be pineapples. It's important not to go for the canned variety which could contain unhealthy preservatives. You will want the fresh kind of pineapple.

Be careful not to just rely on pineapple juice, though. Consuming the fruit isn't just a sweet and refreshing treat. It also enriches your endocrine glands. Many experts believe that pineapples are also a source of psychic energy, helping you clear your mind as you tap into your intuition.

Another suitable choice is broccoli. Scientists have found that organic broccoli helps stimulate the operation of your endocrine glands. When these are healthy, your body becomes better at releasing hormones into your bloodstream, immediately alerting you of your intuitions.

On a more nutritional level, you will also want to get a good dose of vitamins A and D at the same time. These nutrients are known to interact well with your endocrine system, allowing for a better synthesis of your hormones.

In that sense, almond nuts and Brazil nuts are ideal sources of this combination. Couple those with daily intakes of dairy products such as milk and cheese, and you have a healthy set of endocrine glands.

13 - The Intuitive Dreamer

Most people simply dismiss dreams and patched-up scraps of memories that seem to bind themselves together when you sleep. For the intuitive individual though, dreams play a very significant role when it comes to understanding their emotions.

This is probably the reason why intuitive people enjoy vivid dreams more often than most people. When you dream of something good, you sense every details and take away the joy long after you wake up.

The same thing can be said about nightmares. They glare into your being and haunt you with their mysterious meanings even when you're no longer sleeping. This is why gifted intuitive people pay very close attention to their dreams. Once you learn how to read your dreams, their messages will empower you and help you live your gifted life to the fullest.

Dream Interpretation

Fortunately, you don't need a third eye or years of experience as an empath or psychic to understand what your dreams mean for you. All you need is some basic knowledge and some simple recording tools.

With that said, the most important thing you'll need is your journal. How can you analyze a dream if you don't write it down? Sadly, humans are prone to forgetting most of their dreams a few minutes after they wake up. Intuitive people, however, can maintain these memories after they're awake, allowing them to better recall them when the time comes.

Keep your journal beside you when you go to sleep. When you wake up from a dream, reach for the journal and scribble down what happened in your dream.

Don't try to immediately dissect your dream as you write. The goal is to get as much of what you've dreamed onto paper for later inspection. Do not worry about being chronologically correct of the events that take place in your dreams. You will want to get as many details as possible.

What To Ask Yourself

After a dream as well as your efforts to write them in your journal, find time within the day to sit down with your work. There, go over the things that transpired in your mind and try to see if you can play things back based on your notes.

As you go over these notes, ask yourself some questions which will help you discern what your subconscious is trying to tell you.

What was the theme?

Look back at your memory of the dream and try to see if there was a general theme for what happened. Here, you try to determine if you had a good dream or bad dream.

Each event that took place in your dream revolves around a certain effect. Despite being unorganized and chaotic, our subconscious still manages to organize our dreams around a central concept. Were you dreaming of a celebration? A test? An attack? A death? A romance? Zero in on that concept.

To help you answer that question, try to take apart various elements of your dream and ask yourself more specific questions. Where were you in the dream? Are you familiar with the place? Who was with you? What were you doing with these people? Was there anything happening to you?

Were you reliving a good memory? Or a bad one? Try to factor our details that are too hazy for you to remember and focus on the things that came vividly. Did any particular object or person stand out from the things that happened in your dream?

As you answer this question, write your sentiments down as well. Those will soon come together in the form of a message as you complete your dream analysis.

What was the predominant emotion?

What was the general mood of the events that took place in your dream? Don't just try to remember what mood the people and atmosphere had. Look back and try to determine what emotions you yourself were feeling in your dream?

Don't just say happy if you were happy. Here is where things get interesting. Try to rationalize the way you were feeling in your dream. If you felt happy during the dream, try to tell yourself why you were feeling that way.

Was it because you were with someone? Was it because something favorable to you was happening in your dream? Was it because of the other people involved in the dream?

Did you win something? Did you get rid of something? Try to a "why" to what you were feeling.

Even if you were feeling something negative, it's still important to rationalize. If you were feeling terrified by your dream, try to zero in on what triggered your fear. Were you being attacked? Was someone close to you being attacked? Was something important to you being destroyed? Were you the one being destroyed? Was something being taken from you?

Answering these questions will help you understand a little more about yourself. Perhaps there is something that you can't admit to yourself when you're awake which causes your subconscious to reflect your true sentiments while you sleep.

What symbols were present in the dream?

Don't just look for insignia, flags, and signs in your dream. The word "symbol" can be a very vague term at times.

When looking for symbols, look for things, actions, gestures and even people that stuck out to you. An important symbol in your dream is one that usually stands out the most and is what you can immediately recall when you wake up.

Were you at the amusement park? Did you ride nothing but the roller coaster? Were you celebrating someone's birthday or wedding? Did you give them something? Was something given to you?

Were you with someone in your dream? What were you doing with this person? What was this person doing to you? What does this person mean to you?

Sadly, there are no defined sets of characteristics to tell you what makes a symbol in your dream. It's more of a personal question. What was symbolic to you? What element of your dream do you believe signifies something that translates into your waking world?

When you've found your symbols, be sure to write them down and highlight their seeming importance to you. Don't worry if you can't put a finger on their significance yet, the activity isn't over.

How are all these elements connected?

When you have the theme, symbols, and emotions written down, you're ready to start digging deep.

Put on your thinking cap and awaken the left side of your brain. Here, you're also going to need logic to put everything together in a central message. Take the various elements you've dissected and try to piece them together into one central message. What are these things, feelings, people and emotions trying to tell me?

Take, for example, a dream about you standing in front of a classroom, without any clothes on.

The first and most striking emotion you'll experience is a shame. The embarrassment will almost overwhelm you. This shame is symbolic for you because it stands out the most.

Take this as a sign that you might be walking into an embarrassing situation. It could be at work or with your friends and family. Whatever it is, the shame will almost be unbearable.

Take it as your brain trying to tell you what you're going to feel if you don't take action. Try to remember the people laughing and you and pointing at you as you stand in front of them naked. It's all one big symbol revolving around the concept of shame that puts you in the spotlight.

Take note that this is not the only rationale behind interpreting dreams. It happens to be a very personal experience. It requires a delicate combination of tracing back your past experiences and the sensations you feel as you dream.

Only you can tell the significance of the symbols you encounter in the dream world. This is why it's important to let your thoughts fly as you ponder on the supposed meaning of these symbols to you.

It's important not to force a connection. Just let your thoughts and imagination run lose as you think about it. Make sure your mind is relaxed. It's a good idea to practice some mindfulness meditation right before engaging in this activity.

This is where the final step and question comes in. What actionable course can I take?

Once you have the message, what are you going to do about it? Once you have the interpretation, it's time to put things into action. It's time to take the subconscious message and place it in your conscious plans.

Going back to your humiliating example, you can start by either reviewing any work you might have submitted or will yet be submitted. Double check if you've made any grave errors that could cost you your competence.

Don't just take a look at your work. Go back on your social media newsfeeds and post and see if you haven't been making a fool of yourself in front of other people on the internet.

14 - Conclusion

As you complete this manual, notice that you've become more comfortable with yourself and your talents. Congratulations on reaching a new level of appreciating your gift!

The first thing you will want to do after this is to get your journal. If you have one already prior to this manual, go ahead and write about your experience reading this book. What points struck close to home? What new concepts were introduced? What new discoveries did you make about yourself?

If you're only starting a journal after this book, make your first entry a special one by committing to writing in it every day.

Don't just set aside a certain time of day in which to write. Commit to writing what goes on in your heart and in your mind the moment something interesting happens to you. Write in it the moment you are plagued by your emotions and instinct.

What's important here is that you begin to like writing in your journal. It won't solidify as a habit if you don't appreciate what it does for you.

For your first entry, write about how you feel, now that you've uncovered much of this great talent that lies deep inside you. Does it empower you to become more confident? Or does it confuse you to think that you still have much to learn? No matter what you're feeling, root yourself in the moment and register it to memory.

When you've done that, it's time to go out into the world and share your gifts with the people who matter most. You may have family members already going through something that needs your understanding and advice. You may have friends that need a listening ear. Go out and build those bonds to further empower your talents.

Also, don't forget that you're not the only gifted intuitive individual on the planet. Seek like-minded and like-gifted people. Meet them and learn from them. You will be amazed at how deep and complex other intuitive people can be from the eyes of another intuitive person.

On the same note, don't be afraid to share what you know about your gift to other individuals that are struggling with their intuition. Be a beacon for them and show them the path to truly enjoying the gift.

14 - CONCLUSION

Congratulations once again!

Book 2 - Setting Boundaries

Learn When To Say Yes And No (Difficult People, Empath, Saying No, Survival Manual, Toxic People)

1 - Introduction

You, as an empath, possess an extraordinary gift. That is the ability to understand the emotions of others far better than anyone else. You're naturally sensitive, which allows you to perceive things on a completely different level.

Of course, people with such innate talent are also bestowed with big hearts. You don't just understand how most people feel. In your own special way, you can feel what others feel as well. Their pain, joy, triumphs, and suffering become your own.

In line with this gift, you are driven by the need to help others. You relish in the happiness of the people around you and you wallow with them in their sorrows.

But this doesn't make you a mind reader. You're human, after all. You have your own limitations. There are still things you cannot do, no matter how much you want to help someone.

And because you're sensitive to others, you're also vulnerable. You're susceptible to abuse and the dependence of others. This, in turn, may stress you out and turn your gift into a burden that you carry for the rest of your life.

This is where this manual comes in. Here, you will learn to protect your gift and prevent it from becoming a problem. You will develop skills that will counteract your weaknesses and help bring out a better version of yourself.

2 - What are Boundaries?

The dictionary defines 'boundary' as a blockade. It's something that keeps something in, or everything else out, for that matter. In other entries, boundaries are defined as a distinct point where one thing ends and another begins. It is an indicator of limitations.

But what does that mean for a gifted individual such as yourself? Have you ever heard of boundaries for people with talents such as the ones you have?

Empath Boundaries

You know that your talents revolve around your sensitivity – your ability to feel what other people are feeling, sometimes, even better than they do.

This means you understand people on a completely different level. Relating to others is second nature to you. You take their emotions and thoughts and make them your own, without having to ask them for it.

Because of this natural ability, it also becomes natural that you want to help other people. Deep down, you understand that by alleviating the emotional distress of the person you're with, you also feel their worries dissipate.

But that talent comes at a price: your own sensibility.

What happens to you when you're surrounded by the negativity of others every day? What will become of you when the whole world disrupts your calm with worries from those people around you?

How will you respond to a sea of people clamoring for your attention and understanding? Who will you help? Who will you turn down? Whose disappointment is more bearable? Why should all of this even be a concern of yours?

When the pressure and the routine negativity starts to set in, what do you do? Are you to play the martyr and dedicate yourself to every call that needs your help? Or are you to play the unforgiving teacher, protecting yourself and your interests from the influence of others?

Where does your need to help end and where does your duty to protect yourself begin? When is it ok to say that you've given enough of yourself to a certain cause?

Where do you draw your boundaries? You may know what

they are but how do you protect yourself from the weight of the world and still enjoy your gift?

The Importance of Boundaries

Despite your gifts and talents, you're still human. Yes, you have the capacity for great love and affection, but that love has to start with yourself. How will you be an emotional stronghold for others when you can't even protect yourself from the weight other people are carrying?

Yes, it's in your nature to help, but up to what point? When does help turn into abuse? When does assistance turn into complete dependence? Sometimes, helping out too much doesn't become helping anymore.

And it's not just with helping other people. What about people that don't want help? What about those people that are already happily on their way towards self-destruction?

Or worse, what about those people that think they know better than you? What about people that are out there to take advantage of you? You may not like it, but your gifts allow you to see through their facade, showering you in their negativity. What if you deal with this every day?

This is where boundaries come in. At some point, you have to draw the line somewhere. Being the talented empath that you are, even drawing a line has to be done carefully. This is because there are many things to consider:

Your Welfare

This should stand out more than anything else. You won't be any good to anyone if you yourself is damaged beyond repair. You may think you're strong, but even the strong need to rest from time to time.

The Ones Closest To You

These are the people that matter most to you. They may or may not be family to you, but their presence in your life brings you positivity and enlightenment. These people care about you just as much as you care about them.

Toxic People

Why are these people part of the considerations? Aren't they just there to ruin your mood? On the contrary, these people are what make you strong. Although living or dealing with a toxic person every day is bad for you, they are necessary if you want to become tougher yourself.

That may seem like an easy list, but ticking off each item can be more difficult than expected.

Sometimes, we tend to get caught up in our daily lives that we end up exhausted on a physical and emotional scale. When this happens, everything and anything can affect you.

When you've spent the day being a gift to other people, you don't notice that you're giving too much of yourself away. In turn, you end up letting yourself go.

Without proper care of your own skills and emotions, you could end up despising your gift, putting it away as you join non-gifted people in a sea of untapped emotions. In fact, your behaviors right now could be an indicator of what is to come.

The Signs of Deterioriation

Yes, life may seem good at the moment. You have a career and a family and a group of friends. That sounds good and all, but have you reviewed the status of the relationships that you already have? Have you stopped to think what kind of relationship you have with the people around you?

Try to review the relationships that you have right now and be on the lookout for the following signs:

1. Are you expected to drop your commitments on account of the needs of others? Have the people around you become accustomed to your availability that they become upset when your schedule doesn't coincide with theirs?

2. Is 'yes' your default answer to most requests? Are you bypassing your own emotional checks before committing to something just for the sake of helping someone? Do you find it difficult to leave someone to their devices even if you feel like helping them is going to inconvenience you?

3. Do you feel emotionally drained around the people who are supposed to nourish and empower your talents? Have they now become sources of toxicity instead of positivity for you?

4. Are your efforts to help others belittled? When was the last time you felt the warmth of gratitude from

someone you helped? Do people just see you as a listening ear or a source of comfort? Are you only relevant when someone needs you?

These signs will tell you if you're living in a downward spiral. Have you trained other people into believing the unrealistic notion that you are at their beck and call? Have they been convinced that your sole purpose in life is to see to it they're OK?

You may feel like you can take on anything right now, but your needs will eventually surface. When that happens, multiple emotional dissonances take place. Relationships will get cut off. You'll end up feeling lost and defeated.

Of course, you don't want that to happen. This is why you have to set boundaries. These will allow you to enjoy your gifts and in turn, enjoy the life you've chosen for yourself, along with the people that are important to you.

Challenges

Although setting boundaries is an important part of your life, this is easier said than done. Unlike physical boundaries, empath boundaries are slightly trickier because of a few things.

First, it's difficult for you to turn off your talents. When you walk down a crowded hallway full of other people, you can't help but immerse yourself in that sea of emotions.

This can even be a sickening experience if you have the misfortune of walking within the vicinity of very toxic people. You can't help but be affected by their thoughts and emotions which come at you like a giant wave of sensations – all demanding to be felt at the moment.

And you know better than anyone that you can find toxic people everywhere, even at home. You may have found yourself taking the high-road most of the time at home, understanding and adjusting to the people around you. But even high roads run out.

When that happens, being at home becomes more draining than being someplace else. You would rather delay going home, spending more time at work or finding other people that provide you with a more comfortable environment. This, in turn, puts a strain on the relationships you have with your family.

So at the very core, it's a simple question with many possible answers. How will you, someone with the capacity to understand and feel the same way as everyone, let everyone know that you cannot be that someone all the time?

3 - Understanding Energy Ties

Part of appreciating and controlling your gift is understanding how it operates. That may be difficult if you do not have a mental framework on which to project your ideas.

It's also inherently difficult to answer the question of how does your empath ability work. Are your experiences the same as those of other empaths in other places? What exactly happens when you start picking up on the feelings of other people?

Energy Ties

This is where the model of energy ties comes in. This model claims that empaths establish ties with the people around them. These are invisible ties made of energy relationships that connect the empath and a certain person.

Think of these ties as invisible threads that you attach to certain people. By making these energy ties, you declare that you exert energy on these people and they do the same unto you.

These ties are created when you bond with someone. This could be through having a cup of coffee with someone, having a long talk with a friend, sleeping with your partner, and even the simple act of having dinner with your family.

Imagine these ties as conduits that transfer energy. In most cases, that energy will come from you and go towards the other person. This is what can drain you.

Imagine someone toxic in your life. Try to visualize your current energy tie to them. Is it just a one-way stream that continually eats from you? These are the ties that damage you. You keep on radiating energy but you get none in return.

On the other hand, two-way energy ties are very enriching for you. Do you have a connection like that in your life? These are people who give as much as they take in terms of emotional support. When you're with these individuals, you feel comfortable sharing your insights. You also get useful insights from them as well.

These are usually people that also care about you. This care and affection flow back to you within your energy ties with them. Dealing with these kinds of people is a joy for you, as you'll never seem to run out of energy while you bond with them.

The Nature of Energy Ties

Apart from being conduits of emotions and energy, a few more things can be said about energy ties.

For one, energy ties are made unconsciously. That is, you're not made aware of the presence of a certain connection until it's already been established. Unfortunately, this means you're unable to dictate when to establish one. This is how some empaths end up physically- and emotionally-drained with all the one-way connections they've let out of control.

One very good example of this property occurs the moment someone is born. This is where you create your first energy bond. Naturally, that's with your biological mother. Even before you can create your own thoughts and fend for yourself, your natural talents are already at work for you.

Another thing to note about these ties is that you can have them with anyone or anything. This means you may also have ties with objects and even people that are no longer alive.

Do you still feel certain pangs of regret and anxiety when you speak about a departed person? Do you become emotionally-charged when someone talks about your favorite band or singer? These are indicators that you've created an energy tie with these things and people.

This may (or may not) make things more manageable for you as an empath. It's more of a personal question. How do you manage your energy ties to something that can no longer adjust to you or something that is outside your influence?

Another thing to note is that these energy ties don't necessarily have to have a physical basis or foundation. That means you don't need to come into physical contact with someone to create an energy tie.

Interestingly, you can also create bonds with people you've never met. Was there an author whose work has spoken to you on a deep and meaningful level? You've probably created a tie with them through their works.

In addition to that, the stronger your feelings are towards someone or something, the stronger the effect of these energy ties. Have you ever disliked a certain person's aura to a high extent? Even if you don't want to, you've created an energy link with them.

In that case, have you ever felt nauseated when this person is simply in the same vicinity as you? Have you ever been surprised by how affected you are by this other person or thing? You may not have noticed, but your energy ties with this person or thing is affecting you strongly as well.

One final thing you have to understand about energy ties is that they're not permanent, as much as your emotions lead you to believe. These ties dissolve and can even be severed with proper discipline and methods.

Despite that, this attribute only becomes true if you choose it. An energy tie you've established will only be there for as long as you will it. Whether it's a good or bad one for you, only you can decide which stays and goes.

This means it's possible to manage your connections. It just needs plenty of discipline and self-reflection – which you'll be learning throughout this chapter.

Bad Ties and Good Ties

It would be easy for a beginner to assume that all you want are two-way connections that enrich your life as an empath, but it could be more complicated than that.

This is because not all two-way ties are beneficial for you. Take, for instance, a co-worker that shares your disdain for a certain supervisor. Imagine this disdain to have mutated to the point that you and your colleague are both contemplating an immature resignation without any backup plans.

Imagine this shared hatred that two of you have towards this common enemy. As an empath, you feed off this hatred coming from your friend, further fueling your own emotions. In the end, the two of you enable each other to a certain extent. This could lead the two of you to the unemployment office ahead of time.

You may be blinded by your current mood, but when the paychecks stop coming in, you would have wished you had better control over your temper. This is a real-life situation that happens on a daily basis to many empaths that only see the value of these two-way ties.

But even with that notion, there is no golden rule which states which ties are good and which are bad. This tends to be a very personal question, which is why it requires plenty of self-reflection.

This is why this question has to be answered with a calm

mind. Making decisions while you're emotionally-charged is going to lead to irrational decisions that may hurt you in the long run.

Take a look at both your emotional and physical state when deciding what is good and bad for you. Sometimes, a one-way tie is easier to deal with compared to a two-way tie in the sense that you don't get carried away with your emotions. As they always say: too much of a good thing is always bad.

Make sure that you set aside time to determine which ties stay and which ones should go. This may seem like a simple discussion with yourself that could take just a few minutes, but in reality, it should take much longer.

Give yourself a good half hour to dilute your thoughts. That requires concentration and meditation. As an empath, you should already know how important it is to make decisions with a clear mind.

Severing Ties

Once you've gone through the process of determining which ties should stay in your life and which ones should go, it's time to liberate yourself from what is holding you back.

This process will require sincere effort and plenty of retrospection. Simply affirming that you no longer have an energy tie with someone or something may sound like a quick fix, but it won't solve the problem permanently.

The first thing you have to do is to accept the presence of the tie and recognize its presence in your life. If it's a toxic tie, this may be difficult as this process may cause negative feelings and memories to surface. You have to toughen yourself and maintain a clear mind with the knowledge that once you're done, this tie will bother you no longer.

Sit yourself down and close your eyes. Picture the person or object or memory to which this tie is attached. Now, visualize a visible connection between you and this object. Try to paint a mental picture of this tie you have created.

Be creative with your visualizations. Is this tie a string? A cord? Perhaps a long strand of bloody barbed-wire? Bring to mind the kinds of feelings this tie brings you and give it a physical form inside your mind.

Now, don't just give this tie form, give it life. Different ties bring in different kinds of emotions and thoughts to you. Is this tie vibrating quite vigorously out of anger? Is this tie drooping very low because it is draining you? Is it twisting and turning as if to confuse you and lead you astray? Be honest with yourself and bring this tie to life in your mind.

If you have intentions of severing this energy tie, this mental image should reflect the very reason why you want to get rid of it. Is it hurting you? Is it demoralizing you? Is it draining you? Turn this visual image into a representation of what this tie is doing to your life. This may become an unpleasant experience at first, but it is a necessary part of the process.

With this mental image in mind, slowly say to yourself "it is there". Recognize its presence and do not deny it. This threat is real in your life. It is keeping you from happiness and comfort.

Next, ask yourself, "Who put it there?"

You know the answer to that question, but don't blame yourself. You cannot stop yourself from creating ties. It's part and parcel of the talents that you possess. Not a lot of people can create what you've made.

As you answer this question, you may begin questioning your gifts. How could you have become attached in such a manner? Where is your self-discipline? How could you have let things get out of control?

Do not blame yourself. Everyone makes mistakes. Remember what you're trying to accomplish right now. You've found the problem. You're now trying to fix it. And now, you have a full image of the problem in all its splendor. It's time to remove it from your life.

With this vivid visual image already in your head, dive into the root of the relationship. Why is this tie doing this to you? What happened to you when you created this tie?

Was this tie created when someone hurt you? Was this energy bond created from a feeling of desperation or loneliness? Go back to the time you encountered this person or object or memory and take a good look at yourself. What were you feeling during that time?

With this feeling in mind, begin to remind yourself why you don't need this feeling anymore. Visualize this root and picture yourself addressing this tie at its very core. You do not need to feel this way anymore. You are no longer dependent on this sensation.

In this case, you may begin to question such an affirmation. How can you say something like that?

Here, you draw on your talents and say this affirmation:

"I no longer need to feel this way because I can create better bonds with better people."

You can do better. You always can. You've probably done so already. At this point, draw energy from the other things in your life that are good for you. Next to the image of the tie you want to remove, place a happy memory or the image of something that has been good to you. Think of a positive tie that you already have in your life. Do the same thing you did with the tie that you want to remove.

Now draw energy from this tie. Use it to fuel your affirmations. You no longer need the other energy tie. You can make better ones. You already have a better one. Visualize this energy interfering with the tie you want to sever. Imagine it blocking out the influence of the tie, causing it to dissolve.

With this, imagine your pain, grief, shame, anger, and other emotions slowly dissolve as well in the light of your positive relationships. Make your talents work for you. Draw energy from what gives you happiness and use it to sever these negative ties in your life. Make them dissolve.

It's important not to put any negative connotations as this happens. Don't visualize yourself destroying the tie or violently cutting it. This will only breed negativity in your mind, further empowering the tie you want to remove. Cutting energy ties shouldn't be a violent process.

It's a gentle realization that there is so much more to you than this tie. It's the acceptance that you can create something that damages you and enriches you as well. It's forgiving yourself for what you've made and appreciating what you can accomplish at the same time.

This immense amount of energy is more than enough to dissolve the ties you want to remove.

As you slowly visualize this tie drifting into nothingness, you will also realize that you feel lighter. With the same image still there, you will feel less, perhaps even nothing at all. This is a sign that the process of cutting this tie is working for you.

As you open your eyes, take in a deep breath and fill yourself with positivity from the remnants of the images you conjured. This is how you cut a tie that you will no longer need.

This is a very powerful process that can eliminate self-doubt in your talents and it should be used only when you're mentally prepared. If you have a shred of doubt in your mind, then this process will do nothing for you.

On top of that, you may need more than one sitting to fully sever some other ties. This could be because of your attachment to these ties are very strong or because they were born from traumatic events from which you still haven't moved on.

4 - Saying No

An empath's life is full of empowerment. The very premise of your talents focuses on empowering yourself and those around you. By drawing in emotions and energy from other people, you become stronger. By being an emotional anchor that fully understands other people, you make others become stronger as well.

This means your life will be full of "yes!" statements that unleash motivation and positivity. On good days, you feel that you can take on anything that comes your way.

But that is far from reality. You're still human. You have limits. In a sea of demands and pleas for your energy and attention, will you say yes to everything that comes your way?

That is a recipe for disaster and misery. One of the most painful truths an empath must face is the fact that they cannot handle everything and they cannot help everyone.

This will go against your natural humanitarian nature. You want to help people, that's part of who you are – and you're in one of the best positions to do so. But it is important to remember that your well-being comes first. How can you help others when you're unable to help yourself?

The Choice

Just like many other things in your life, the option of rejecting an idea, request, or opportunity is a very personal question. There is no golden rule to consider here.

No one else decides the value something should hold for you other than yourself. As an empath, you cherish that value even if no one else sees it.

Your family may question your decision to live with an unemployed painter. What they see is a burden but you may see a passionate artist waiting for a good break. No one else can tell you if your family is right or wrong. That's a distinction you have to make for yourself.

Fortunately, there are a few guidelines you can use to find a good balance in the people and things that you accept in your life.

5 - Self-Preservation

This should be at the top of your considerations. Will something hurt you? You may call it selfish to think of your welfare before that of others, but you have to remember that your gift flourishes when you are well. How can you use your talents if you're marred in misery and pain?

When something or someone threatens your well-being, it's probably best to stay away. You're an empath, not a wall. You're not invincible.

These things will be easy for you to see. Your talents allow you to spot greed, deception, jealousy, malice, and even hate from a mile away. You can tell if someone is genuinely concerned about you or is hiding a different agenda.

You have that gift for a reason. It's also meant to protect you from those that want to take advantage of your natural kindness. These people have no place in your life as they will only be sources of constant toxicity and pain. No matter how high your tolerance is to misery, these people will eventually break you.

The Good of Many

You may not like it, but you will eventually come to choices you think only involve you, but may in truth, affect many other people. Although you're just one special empath, you're surrounded by many other people that will inevitably be affected by the decisions you make.

This is especially true if you have a family of your own. Would you be willing to go on a humanitarian mission to Africa if you already have a toddler about to start school?

Consider the people close to you. In your drive to help others, you may start to ignore the people that need you the most. Or worse, you could end up driving away the people you depend on the most.

Although it's normal to have disagreements with your family and loved-ones from time to time, it's crucial that you're still concerned about their well-being to a certain extent. You cannot expect to relish the joy in helping other people if the very people you love are suffering around you.

Those That Don't Want Help

As an empath, your heart will want to reach out to many people, whether you've met them in real life or not. You might have read about someone on social media or seen something in news that will just make you want to reach out to these people.

Sometimes, these people that you want to help may not want any help at all. Remember, people, differ from one another. You live in a sea of emotions and ideas coming from different backgrounds and principles.

Get used to the fact that there will be people that do not believe you can help them. They will most likely be the same people that do not believe in your talents either. When you're dealing with them, chances are you'll feel a strong sense of self-doubt and skepticism coming from them which could become your own sentiments if you're not careful.

There will be toxic people in your life that will be beyond help, no matter how much you think they can be helped. You may be true in thinking that these people just need more love and understanding, but they may not even be looking for those things at all. They may not even know what they need in the first place.

Will you pick up the phone from a suicidal acquaintance that has been in and out of rehabilitation? What will you tell them if you do so? What if you cannot convince them to give up their plans of ending their own life? Will you carry that burden? What if they just want someone else to feel the misery they're feeling? How will you make them understand that you're already feeling their hopelessness?

Such cases will drain you and depress you. You cannot afford to damage your sensibilities in such a way. On top of that, helping or even attempting to help these kinds of people will just disappoint you in the long run.

The Helpless

If there are people that don't want help, then there will also be those who will want nothing but help. These are the cases that will really speak to you on a frustrating level.

Have you ever had that friend that would constantly ask for relationship advice from you regarding their abusive partner? You would help them by relating to their position and trying to give them the best advice possible.

How would you feel if you see the same friend in the same problem a few weeks after you've talked to them? How would you feel if they did the exact opposite of what you told them to do?

There will be people that just want the attention that comes with pity. They want to feel important but will stick to their own choices when no one is around. When their plans backfire, they will run to you once again for support.

This is just as draining and toxic as someone that doesn't want to be helped. With these people, you will see your energy and emotions go to waste. You will feel fulfilled in approaching them but defeated when you get back to them.

This is because these people possess a skewed perspective of the priorities of other people. For them, they can only make the right choices when other people are coddling them. They feel empowered to do the right thing only when it draws other people close to them.

You may feel a strong need to support these kinds of people, but in the end, you may be the one seeking support from the disappointment you'll experience.

Proper Rejection

Sure, finding a situation wherein saying no is the answer is relatively easy. With the many encounters and decisions you make on a daily basis, the next opportunity to protect yourself might be just around the corner.

But when it's there, how do you do it? As an empath, you know how rejection feels. In a very strange way, you know you will also feel the sting of rejection you're going to give someone the moment you say no to them.

That, in itself, will make you feel horrible as well. This will cause you to reconsider and make a rash decision out of pity and guilt. How does the empath such as yourself rise above this conundrum?

Most experts point out that feeling guilty after a rejection is a sensation that comes from our logical reasoning. We feel guilty when we say no because we think it's the wrong thing and that we're being selfish.

For an empath, that feeling of selfishness and guilt is multiplied several times over. On top of the personal guilt you'll be feeling, you'll also be feeling the vindictive vibes coming from the other person. It's a potent formula for feeling miserable.

But your solution lies in that fact as well. You get rid of the guilt and selfishness if you review your reasons for saying no in the first place.

No, you're not being selfish by saying no. In most cases, saying no is the smart thing to do. This is why it can be difficult for an intuitive empath. This is because you rely on your guts and instincts more than you rely on your logic.

But put your reasoning mind to good use in these instances. As an empath, you will stick with a decision if you feel strongly about it. In fact, that is the only way you know how to make decisions. It's either you're truly convicted or you're truly dejected from someone or something.

Draw that confidence from reasoning. Before you say no, you're sure to always weigh things out. Will this decision be good for me? Will helping this person result in someone becoming better off because of my influence? Is this person just trying to take advantage of me? How well do I know this person? Can I trust them with my attention and effort?

Once you've answered those questions for yourself, then you make a decision. When you give your answer, stick to what you've done before making that decision. You're not saying no because you're selfish and you have better things to do. You're saying no because that is the right thing to do. And you of all people will side by what's right for everyone.

Remind yourself of this notion the next time you have to say no to someone. When the feeling of guilt starts to set in, immediately clear your mind and remind yourself that you are doing the right thing by protecting yourself and the people close to you by saying no.

Another important thing that you have to remember is never to beat around the bush. Keeping things hanging out of fear of encounters is only going to prolong your suffering and add more reasons for you to say yes out of pity.

When someone asks you for something, give your answer right away if you've already thought about it.

On the other hand, if you need more information, be specific about how much time you need to think about things.

On top of that, tell them when they can expect an answer from you. The clearer your guidelines are, the less guilt you'll feel for taking your time as you make your decision.

Most experts say giving an answer within the day is the most polite way to go. Of course, there are cases wherein major decisions might take more than a day, especially if these decisions and requests require large amounts of money or the assistance of other people. Be clear about what you need to do in order to make your decision.

Difficult People

Despite your best efforts, not everyone will appreciate rejection from you. That's something that is out of your control. With that being said, it shouldn't affect you on any level.

But another point of concern here are the people that simply will not take no for an answer. If there are people that can take your rejection and go away, there will also be people that will lie and threaten you to get what they want.

These are the kinds of people that will do you no good. Despite your best efforts to be sincere and thoughtful of their feelings, they will try to manipulate you into agreeing with them. As an empath, you will be able to sense that right away. When that happens, be prepared for a little encounter.

And no, you shouldn’t back down from such people. Their temperament and attitude is all the more reason to stick with your rejection of them in the first place. If these people cannot respect your reasons and decisions, then you have no business in dealing with them in any form or level.

When this happens, go back to your reasons. What these people will do is try to change your perspective and make you see things through a distorted version which they have created just for you.

Remember that whatever they say is not the entirety of your situation. It is just one aspect usually the selfish and self-serving aspect. Do not be swayed by what they say and how they act. If they are not mature enough to handle your decision, then that is their problem. The maturity of other people is something that you cannot fix, no matter how hard you try.

If you have to explain yourself to them, then do so. Lay out your reasons to them and tell them that you’re saying no because it is the right thing for you. If they tell you otherwise, tell them that that is their own perspective of the situation.

You will have to be ready for plenty of aggression and other negative emotions coming your way as this happens. People not used to being rejected will immediately fill with a sense of vindictiveness and anger towards you. You will be feeling that during your encounter.

Take strength from the fact that you are dodging a bullet and protecting yourself. Remember that once the encounter is over, so should your feelings of guilt and selfishness. You're not a benevolent being. You're just a kind-hearted empath.

There will also come a time that these people will not leave you alone. Your explanations will mean nothing to them and they will pester you to change your mind. In these cases, taking your leave is the key. Do not stick around to give them any more opportunity to intoxicate you with their behavior.

Tell them that this is the last you'll speak of this issue with them and take your leave. Excuse yourself properly as to let them know that you no longer wish to speak with them about this matter. Once you do that, there is no other socially-acceptable way to keep you attached to that situation.

6 - Grounding

On top of proper rejection and recognition of energy ties in your life, another boundary you must make for you lies within your own reasoning patterns.

Empaths are known to be very prone to sensation overloads as well as mental breakdowns. These usually happen when you've had too much to handle. The worst part about this is that these breakdowns are usually because your boundaries are weak.

One good way to strengthen these boundaries is by grounding yourself. Similar to the way the ground neutralizes incoming currents, you need to establish a neutralizing plane in your mind where your fears, thoughts, and concerns just cancel each other out.

That may sound like a difficult thing to do, but all you need is the proper method. Fortunately, there are many ways to do that.

This is because the goal of grounding is to hit the brakes on your mental and emotional activity. Think of it as an emergency stop that will bring you back to reality.

The main premise of grounding is to put you in a state of neutrality so that you can better gauge what you're feeling. It affords you the opportunity to check your thoughts and emotions and to put a damper on anything that could escalate into depression and anxiety.

Finding Your End

One very big aspect of grounding is the notion of delineating your personal feelings from the sensations that you pick up from other people.

Your talents allow you to pick up and feel what other people are feeling. With that being said, it's easy to get lost in the mesh of emotions when plenty of them start flooding you.

When this happens, you make flawed associations and attachments that bring out, even more, emotions from you. This, in turn, will overwhelm you despite the fact that everything about you should be fine.

Where do your emotions end? Where do the influences and vibes from other people begin?

Again, that is a personal question that rests on your capacity to differ one sensation from another. That is something that takes practice. The only way for you to develop the skill of sifting through your emotional plate is by filling it with the emotions of other people.

You might have experienced the need for grounding at certain points in your life. Did you feel a sudden swell of anger as you were walking past a courthouse? Have you ever been attacked by a sudden stir of lust as you passed by a brothel?

Were these feelings very strong? Did you take them on as your own? Did you relate these feelings to a past experience or relationship? This could lead you to believe that you yourself, are creating those emotions.

Your natural talents allow you to pick up emotions from people you haven't even met as well. These emotions become more intense when you interact and bond with these people. But when these feelings start to get the better of you, grounding yourself will be the only break you have.

Fortunately, there are many ways for the talented empath to remain grounded.

7 - Meditation

One of the most effective approaches to grounding is, of course, goal-oriented meditation.

Many people believe that meditation is a religious activity that requires you to join a certain sect or organization before you can reap the benefits of this practice, but this is very far from the truth.

At the very core, meditation is a spiritual exercise and not a religious one. It is something almost everyone can do, regardless of their religious affiliation. So no, you don't have to give up your current set of beliefs just so that you can meditate.

The confusion comes from popularized notions of meditation. Upon hearing the word, do you begin to imagine hordes of monks sitting quietly in the wilderness? Do you visualize holy men from various backgrounds chanting strange mantras with their eyes closed? Although these are legitimate mental pictures of the art of meditation, there's more to it.

Many experts believe in the therapeutic prowess of meditation. Being able to inspect your mind on your own is such a great skill to have; this is what makes meditation your best grounding tool.

Although there are religious forms of meditation, you can practice a universal form that is appreciated and applicable to any religion. This is called Mindfulness meditation.

This form of meditation revolves around the idea of clearing your thoughts and emotions and rooting yourself in the moment – where you are and what is going on around you.

The most basic practice with mindfulness is a simple breathing exercise that will help you cope with a sudden spur of external emotions.

When you feel the need to ground yourself, find a quiet spot on which you can meditate. Usually, a small corner in your office or your bedroom will suffice. When picking a spot, it's important that no one disturbs you as you meditate as it requires concentration on your thoughts.

It doesn't have to be a large space, either. A simple area with a comfortable chair is good enough. Ideally, you will want a chair with a backrest so that you can rest your head as you move through the process.

As you sit yourself down, try not to worry if you're feeling a huge influx of negativity from other people. You will be getting rid of these external disturbances in a while.

As you sit down and relax, begin by taking in one deep breath. As you do, slowly close your eyes as you exhale. This deep breath begins the process of meditation.

Shift your attention to the next breath you will take. At this point, you have successfully transferred the act of breathing from an unconscious activity to a conscious process. You now have to tell yourself to breathe.

In this state, draw a mental picture in your head of your breathing process. Imagine placing a camera into each breath you take. How does it travel towards you? Imagine the journey your breath takes. Imagine it going through your nostrils and into your lungs.

Imagine each breath mixing in with your blood, revitalizing your body. Don't rush your breathing, though. You want to take things as slowly as possible. Feel your lungs expand and collapse with each breath you take. It is important to make clear images of this process in your mind.

As all of this is taking place, you are clearing your mind of everything that was bothering you before you started meditating. Your sole focus is now on your breathing and nothing else. This is a good start.

Despite a good start, your thoughts may start wandering off in different directions as you begin to relax. This is a normal occurrence for many beginners. When this happens, give yourself a gentle reminder that you should only be focusing on your breathing. Guide yourself back to where you started and repeat the process from the beginning.

This whole process should take no more than five minutes of your time. When you are ready to end the meditation process, don't open your eyes immediately. Imitate the slow start you had earlier. Take one last deep breath and imagine it nourishing your body. Hold this breath for a few seconds before exhaling. When you do so, slowly open your eyes.

As you return to your senses, you will notice that you're now relaxed. A successful session will leave you calm and with a clean emotional slate. If you did it right, you'll no longer be feeling the same way you were feeling before you started.

Take note that this can be done at any time, as long as you

can find a quiet place in which to meditate. You don't need any special materials; just a comfortable chair.

It's the most accessible tool for you in this modern world of distractions. For beginners, it may take longer to completely root themselves in the moment, but with practice, mindfulness meditation will become one their greatest assets as an empath.

8 - Creativity

Another way to ground yourself is through artistic release. You may not know it, but empaths make for amazing artists. This is because you literally have more emotional baggage with which to create. On top of fueling your inspiration with your personal experience, you can also tap into the feelings of other people for inspiration.

What's great about the creative arts is that it has many channels and forms. In order to ground yourself most effectively with art, you have to find a medium that appeals to you the most. This, by far, is the most satisfying personal question you can answer for yourself. Through what means will you express yourself?

Will you cling to words and write? Will you pick up the brush and paint? Or the pencil to draw? You can also choose to strum the guitar or any other musical instrument for that matter. What's important is that the method you choose appeals to you and provides you with the creative and artistic release that you need as an empath.

What makes artistic creation an effective grounding tool is the fact that it allows you to tackle with your emotions in a productive manner. You deal with these emotions in creative ways that result in something that adds value to you as a person.

Despite that, you may not have an easy time starting. This is especially true if you haven't entrenched yourself in the arts for the longest time. It's even harder if you've been living all this time trying to boost your career instead of finding an artistic hobby.

This is why it's best to pick up something simple at the beginning. As with every artist, the first step is to always look for inspiration.

This first step should be easy for you. A simple matter of internalization and retrospection should uncover some emotions that are just waiting to be expressed. It's just a matter of zeroing in on this emotion through meditation.

The next thing to do is to find a medium. How do you want to express this emotion? This can be one of the most spiritually satisfying things for an empath. This is because you tend to create energy ties with the things you use. You develop attachments to the tools of the trade.

This may also be a difficult choice. As an empath, you want

to commit to something with all your heart, as with everything. And with a wide array of artistic channels, it can be daunting and confusing to find something that really speaks to you.

If you find yourself stuck in this position, take a step back from your artistic plans and immerse yourself in the creative works of other people. Read a good book. Watch one of your favorite movies. Listen to your favorite songs. Engage in a work of art that speaks to you. More often than not, you find yourself as you experience your own emotions.

Once that's done, it's now just a matter of making the time to commit to your craft.

9 - Humor

You may be surprised to find such a suggestion here, but laughter is, indeed, the best medicine. This goes especially true if you're a gifted empath.

You may have been busy laughing during something hilarious, but what you don't notice is that your body normalizes during this time. Its effect is almost instant, even faster than any breathing exercise or meditation process.

That's the good thing about laughter. It immediately uplifts your spirits and eases out any anxieties you may be harboring at the moment. Despite how effective it is, it is overlooked most of the time because we tend to become too wrapped up in our careers and families.

It's important to let loose sometimes and appreciate the small things that amuse us. You don't necessarily have to find something monumentally funny to become grounded. Sometimes, the minute details work wonders when it comes to making us laugh.

Have you ever left the home just to find out that you put on mismatched socks? Perhaps your underwear is on the wrong way. Noticing these daily oddities is one way to maintain a sense of humor.

Fortunately, we live in a world wherein funny is the new currency. Modify your social media feeds and subscriptions to include things that lighten your mood with laughter. With the never-ending availability of the world through the internet, it's hard to not find things that will make you laugh. It's just a matter of actively looking for what makes you chuckle.

10 - Boundary Magic

Part of any empath life manual is the premise of understanding and enforcing boundaries. This is more than just learning to say no and figuring out where the feelings and emotions of other people begin. In fact, one very big reason why there are many miserable but talented empaths is that they haven't learned how to set boundaries and to enforce them properly.

Boundaries For Empaths

Part of understanding boundaries is appreciating what they are and what they do for people like you. They're not just invisible barriers you put around yourself to protect your feelings from the influences of other people. They're markers of your limitations and capacities. They tell you how much you can love others and how much you should be loving yourself.

The basic premise of boundaries revolves around the notion that despite being capable of great love and help, empaths should also be concerned about loving themselves.

You may also believe the notion that boundaries are something only empaths should practice. On the contrary, everyone should understand boundaries. In fact, you may already have some boundaries in place, you're just not aware that they're there.

Take, for instance, your tolerance of tantrums. If you have a toddler that you bring with you for a meal at a restaurant, what behaviors of this child do you deem acceptable?

It is alright for the toddler to cry when they soil themselves? Is it alright for them to scream in excitement when they see a built-in playpen for children visiting the restaurant?

What if your child is starting to bother other people? What if they begin throwing their food and the utensils around because they cannot eat the food that they want? What if they get up from their seat and run around the restaurant, potentially bumping into waiters and servers as they go about their jobs. Are these behaviors acceptable?

What do you do when this toddler of yours starts to exhibit unacceptable behaviors? How do you discipline them? How do you behave? Do you spank them in public? Do you yell at them in front of other people? Do you immediately ask for the bill and head home to save face? Do you just let them do as they want until they tire themselves out?

You may not notice it, but you have boundaries even in those circumstances. On a fundamental level, boundaries are rules you place for yourself that dictate what behaviors of other people are tolerable for you.

Boundaries also serve as protocols of how you behave when others have crossed their boundaries with you. Do you engage or reason out? Do you permeate in the situation or remove yourself from the encounter? How much of your energy are you willing to spend at this moment?

The Consequences

On top of understanding what boundaries do for you, it's also vital that you appreciate what it means to consistently enforce these boundaries every day. Empaths that have poor boundaries end up with all sorts of problems that they could have solved on their own.

One of the first indications of poor boundaries is self-doubt. When you just let people bypass your boundaries without you doing anything, you will start to question your own motives.

Are you really trying to help someone or do you just want

some comfort from your own insecurities? Are you really there to comfort someone or are you the one that needs help?

You'll start making half-baked decisions that make you feel even more uncomfortable. You'll start to feel that everything is forced out of you and you become a victim of circumstance.

When this occurs, your self-doubt becomes augmented by a shift in your perspective. Instead of caring for yourself and your emotions, you start to consider what other people are thinking of you. The opinions of others begin to weigh on your consciousness, fuelling, even more, doubt in yourself.

This will then cause you to start acting out of tune, going out of your way just to please other people. You begin aiming to get the approval of others by placing your needs on the line.

But in doing so, you develop a fear of confrontation and hearing what other people have to say about you. Despite your efforts to please everyone, you dread coming near them and learning that they don't notice what you do for them.

These things do nothing but fill you with negative emotions, leaving you miserable and helpless. At that point, you wallow and withdraw yourself from other people. Your genuine willingness to help has become a large cloud of self-doubt and unwillingness to be with anyone.

It's strange to imagine that all of these things happen just because you don't stick to your boundaries. Despite this unlikelihood, distinguishing your barriers and enforcing them protects both you and your capacity to be of emotional help to other people. Just like with any gift, yours is something that demands special care.

Different Kinds of Boundaries

At the very core, boundaries protect your integrity as an empath. In line with that, your integrity manifests itself in different planes of existence. With that being said, you have different kinds of boundaries that promote your integrity, keeping you safe in different directions.

Distance

How far away are you from the things that drain your energy? How close are you to the people that give you strength? Do you live with someone toxic? Is there an accessible place of comfort and relaxation to which you can go when the emotions start piling up?

Here, you set your boundaries based on how much you pick up in reference to your location. You may not notice it at first, but placing yourself farther from sources of negativity brings in more light into your perspective. On the same note, being close to bright and positive people makes everything seem like a picnic. Although you can't have a picnic every day, you can come really close to it.

Emotion

In relation to grounding, you have to set boundaries that separate what you feel and what you feel from other people. As an empath, that distinction may be hard to make, especially if you find yourself in the midst of a sea of emotions.

This is why grounding is important for an empath. It's like laying all your cards on the table to see which emotions are yours and which ones come from the people around you.

When you have that knowledge, protecting yourself and your interests become easier. You can avoid people that aren't worth the effort and you prevent the influence of other people from affecting your day. A bad start can easily be turned around into a beautiful day when you learn to separate these emotions and label them appropriate inside and outside your emotional barrier.

Time and Space

These are tricky boundaries to recognize because empaths are big fans of retrospection. You base a lot of your thoughts and plans on things that have happened in the past, particularly those that have affected you deeply.

But here's where a problem arises. Are you learning from the past or are you living in the past?

While it is important to heed lessons from the things that happen to us, to what extent do we let these lessons affect the way we live? Do we create a life fulfilled by knowledge or lead a life led by fear and anxiety?

As an empath, there is no escaping the occasional memory here and there. It's part of who you are. This doesn't necessarily have to be a bad thing; it just requires the proper perspective. Do you let your past guide you or define you?

There's a world of difference right in between that distinction. Take, for instance, a bad childhood experience. Imagine going through the image of being verbally abused during your childhood.

Analyzing such an experience as a child is nearly impossible, given your natural immaturity. But what do you do about it now that you're an adult? Has this experience led you to avoid people that are vocal about their needs? How do you handle other people that are not afraid of confrontation and the inclusive shame of being assaulted verbally?

Do you give in to your childhood anger and prepare a magnificent temper for your family? Do you rise above this experience and set aside your vengeance to become a better parent?

This slight example illustrates your boundaries with time. Moving on from the past or living in it is a choice you can make anytime. Sadly, it's a choice that most empaths fail to make properly. Being people that are driven by emotions more than logic, it's easy to take the path that exudes anger and retribution instead of being the bigger person, which is the main premise of your emotional talents.

And it's not just with the memories you have. You also have boundaries of space to deal with. Where are you right now? Are you home? Does it feel like home? Do you even know what that is?

Go back to the example of an abused childhood. Would you look at home the same way other children do? Home should be a safe haven where you can be yourself and feel secure. Does your abusive childhood lead you to have hesitations about your very home? What do you think of that space in which you live?

What energies do you feel in that area? What energies do you allow yourself to emanate when you are in that space? What general feeling do you associate to the various spaces in your life?

Is work a place of stress or a place of growth? Is home a place of problems or relaxation? Is the company of your friends a chance to enjoy life or to worry about someone else's life?

Take note that these perceptions are all under your control. You decide what associations to make with the spaces in your life. Will you let the past and current experiences dictate how you feel about certain memories and spaces in your life?

Thoughts

One of the most important boundaries you will create is within your thoughts. Most experts delineate a direct relation between your thoughts, emotions, and behaviors. When something is amiss with your thoughts, your behaviors soon follow, disrupting every other boundary you so carefully placed in your life.

This is where your integrity is most at stake – and at the same time, most powerful as well. The boundaries you place on your thoughts mostly dictate how you react to the various things that happen in your life.

Drawing a line between what you think and what others think is one of the first things you have to accomplish if you ever want to help others. How will you help change the thoughts of others when your own cognition are easily dissolved by other people?

A weak set of thought boundaries leads you to believe the things that other people say about you. You know you don't have good boundaries when you cannot think for yourself, leading yourself to count on the cognition of other people. Instead of being of help to others, you become a burden to someone else.

A healthy thought boundary is something that protects the sanctity of your beliefs. Take, for instance, spanking children as a form of discipline.

Although this topic is hotly-debated, you must already have a personal opinion on this. Are you for or against it?

Regardless of your position, do you let the opinions of your own parents and other co-parents affect your belief? Do you let other people dictate how you think about disciplining your children?

It may not even happen with parenting. How about the way you feel about same-sex marriage. It doesn't matter if you're for or against it. What matters is how you let the thoughts of other people affect your stand. Do you even allow the opinions of others in at all?

What if you're dealing with someone who was so vehemently against your principles? How do you deal with their disapproval? Do you take it as a big deal or a big realization of the diversity of people?

The Big Question

With these various boundaries, you have to manage in your life, it's difficult to find a strict set of guidelines that will help you make the right choices.

Again, this issue becomes an intensely personal question that requires much reflection on your end. At the end of the day, you decide what is right for you and what is not. After that, what's required of you is to stick to that belief and wherever it leads you.

How much of yourself are you willing to devote to a certain act? How much of your energy will be allotted to certain people? Are you willing to give a little bit more for special cases? Where do you draw the line on the behaviors of other people?

Boundary Creation

When creating boundaries, it's important to find the time to really sit down with yourself so that you can sort out your priorities and goals.

What do you want to accomplish as an empath? These goals will naturally coincide with your priorities in life. How do you want to enrich the lives of other people? How do you envision the people important to you? Where do you see them after a year or two with your help?

When you have these goals in mind, things become easier. Begin to think about the behaviors and things that will prevent you from reaching these goals.

Do you want to surround your family with an aura of love and affection? Do you want your children to grow up with a sense of wonder and curiosity? Do you wish to see your parents grow old gracefully?

You may also have goals for yourself. Do you want to learn how to reach out to the less fortunate in your area? Are you aiming to become strong enough to weather a terminal disease with a loved one?

These are good goals and all, but what you should focus on are the things that will prevent those things from happening. These could be anything. You could have abusive in-laws or toxic people at work. You might also have school bullies and grades to worry about.

Zero-in on these threats and declare them as unhelpful to you and to those you treasure. But don't just recognize the threat they possess. State in your mind what you will do when these things start influencing your goals.

Will you stand your ground or will you distance yourself from these people and things? Will you try to change the situation or will you change something about yourself?

Remember, you cannot sacrifice the integrity of your personal goals. That's the one boundary that shouldn't go. Up to which point are you willing to deal with your threats? How will you respond to your threats?

In line with that, there are a few things that you can do in order to deal with a present threat to your boundaries.

11 - Posture Manipulation

When something or someone is beginning to cross your boundaries, you will start feeling your energy channel itself towards your response. Will you become submissive or confrontational? Your mind and body will start scrambling for a sense of control under the premise of a threat.

In order to maintain control, change your posture. You'll be surprised that something seemingly mundane as your physical posture can have such an effect on your emotions.

Maintain a powerful stance. You can either cross your arms to delineate your protection of yourself or cross your legs to express your disapproval. These gestures give your body a closed sort of image, empowering the closed state of your mind to the perceived threat to your boundary.

Placing Distance

If the threat still persists, you can also choose to put distance in between you and your threat. Enforcing a boundary of distance keeps your sensitivities safe. The less you see the threat to your boundary, the less you'll feel their influence on you.

Of course, you could be thinking that this is similar to running away from your problem. Rest assured that putting some distance in between yourself and the threat to your boundary is not an act of cowardice so long as you know how to handle it when it is present.

Vocal Rejection

This is where saying no the proper way comes in. If you cannot get away from the threat that is crossing your boundaries, it's time to let them know that you do not appreciate their presence or what they're doing.

This usually means telling someone to back off or to stay away from you. This also means telling someone that you will be having no more of the behavior or presence at this moment. Here is where you set your foot down and stand for the integrity of your boundaries.

This is you letting them know that they are crossing a line and that they should not continue doing so.

In the event that this threat persists without heed to your rejection, it's time to consider the encounter a lost cause. This is where you start walking away. Move yourself to somewhere you're protected.

There's something very powerful about telling someone to back off. The act of projecting your discomfort unto another person who is causing you the discomfort allows you to shift some of your negativity and give it back to them. That way, you don't take their vibes with you when you part ways with this threat.

Sometimes, you may also need to explain yourself to other people. Why is this act crossing your boundaries? What is it that is important to you that you think is under threat by this particular behavior? How are you affected by this?

When you explain your side, be sure to maintain civility in your tone. You do not want to come off as overpowering and intimidating. You are merely protecting yourself, and not imposing your will on someone else. No one can force their will on you unless you allow them to. The same thing can be said the other way around.

Cognitive Affirmations

Sometimes, it's not enough to just say no to someone and back away. Sometimes, some negativity and self-doubt will latch onto you as you walk away, lingering in your mind as you ponder on the encounter.

If left unchecked, these vibes will fester and grow into other violations of boundaries that may happen even when you're far away from your threats.

Have you ever felt bad for saying no to a friend who was desperate to borrow money, even after they've borrowed from you several times already? Did they lash out at you and call you selfish?

As you walked away from this person, did you stop to think that you actually acted selfishly? Did their negativity stick to you even after the encounter?

This is where some positive affirmations of yourself come into play. Do not let these leftover sentiments bother you and cause you to breed some self-doubt.

Remember, you have to protect yourself. Why? Because you are worth protecting. You are worth the trouble. This is an affirmation you give to yourself when you're feeling the sting of a rejection.

Tell yourself that you also have to take care of yourself. You are not delineating yourself as better than someone else. Rather, you are emphasizing the fact that you are valuable enough as a person to practice self-preservation.

Boundary Visualization

On top of telling yourself that you're worth protecting, it helps to create imagery that enforces your value.

Imagine a protective bubble surrounding your person. That bubble is intact thanks to your steadfast rejection and handling of the threats. Imagine what would become of you if this bubble were to burst or become soiled with someone's negativity.

You're keeping that bubble clean because that represents your good intentions. Visualizing this delicate bubble will help put your rejection in the proper perspective. You can't help others if you can't protect yourself.

You have to be strong for yourself before you can start being strong for the other people in your life.

The Harsh Truth

One encounter to a threat may sound exhausting with all the emotional effort and mental processing that has to take place. In fact, you may want to call it a day after properly dealing with one threat to your boundaries.

If life were that simple, everyone would be very happy. Sadly, this is not the case. Defending yourself against one threat to your boundaries may be a good thing, but it's not the only thing that will happen to you in one day.

You will experience a myriad of challenges to your boundaries on a daily basis. Your limits will be tested by the events that happen to you and the by the people that surround you, no matter how much you love them.

You have to be prepared to defend the integrity if your boundaries on a daily basis. This takes precious energy and time to do.

As alarming as that sounds, the empaths that are capable of doing this usually become very remarkable people. Do you know someone like this? Do you know someone you can talk to all the time about your problems as if this other person didn't have any problems of their own?

Is there a strong person in your circle that seems to have everything under control and figured out? That's a person who surely understands their boundaries and has the developed the strength and will to defend their beliefs every day and help those dear to them.

12 - Dealing With Toxic People

Besides learning how to set your boundaries, you also have to learn the reason why boundaries are needed in the first place: the existence of people that cross them.

They are a universal constant, just like change. You wouldn't need boundaries if you could eliminate these people from your life entirely, but that's a far cry from reality.

You will always encounter someone toxic. A good measure of maturity is how you deal with these people in relation to the various boundaries that you have.

But understanding that they exist is not enough. You can't just expect everyone to come into your life is a source of toxicity. There's a lot more to it than meets the eye.

Understanding Toxicity

Why do you call them toxic? What an interesting term to use for these kinds of people. Taking a look at the dictionary, the term "toxic" refers to something poisonous.

If you look at the term "poisonous", it takes on both a figurative and literal meaning. It could refer to something that can cause death or illness when taken into the body. The term is also used to describe something as inherently malicious.

Whatever definition you take for toxicity, one thing is for certain – it makes life unlivable for you as a person. It could either be by their aura or attitude, but a toxic person makes it hard for empaths to function when they're around.

You may already know people like these in your life; these are the people that make things more difficult for you. When you're with these people, you suddenly become drained of energy. You find yourself on the losing end of the stick most of the time.

But a more important question to ask is, what makes someone toxic for an empath such as yourself? What is it about these people that make living around them so difficult?

To answer that, you have to understand the different forms of emotional poisons that these people carry with them.

13 - Types of Toxic People

These people may or may not be aware that they're causing trouble for you. They could be wrapped up in their own issues that they just unconsciously drag people down with them.

On the other hand, there are those that are truly malicious. These are the types of people that really have the intention of doing wrong by you. They could either be driven by a need to stay ahead or they could want something that they think you can provide for them.

As an empath, the first step to dealing with these kinds of people is identifying their presences in your life and labeling the kind of negativity they bring to your existence.

The Manipulative

These people can be the most difficult to identify because of the facade they put on. They will make it a point to know what makes you happy and comfortable. They want you to associate their presence with good times and positivity.

What they do is they will place you in a state of comfort with them so that you drop your boundaries. When they have you right where they want you, that's when they cross your boundaries and ask something of you that will go against your boundaries.

They will use this perceived friendliness to get past your defenses and make you give in to what they want. And when you think of saying no to them, they will guilt you into agreeing with them.

These people understand that they have to play along with you before they can get what they want from you. For that, they are willing to make you believe that you are important to them and then ask you to give proof to this importance.

The Doomed

These people are permanently miserable. Nothing you say or do to them will change the way they feel. Don't mistake them for depressed people, though. These are quite different from those who are clinically inclined to be depressed.

The doomed are people that only know negativity and see to it that everyone sees the same thing they do. They are not easily swayed by positivity because they have a talent for only seeing the bad side of things. For them, there is no silver lining. Everything is bad and you should feel the same.

This is why they'll use sarcasm, anger, mockery, and even guilt to make you feel that your happiness has no place around them. In doing so, they suck out the energy from almost everyone they encounter.

You could start out with a good day but end up frustrated after spending some time with them. Another interesting thing about these people is that they may or may not be aware that they're doing that to the people around them. For them, everything is a sour dish that no one should enjoy.

The Self-Obsessed

In other discussions, these people are known as narcissists. You can also consider them the polar opposite of empaths. If talented empaths such as yourself are capable of sensing and absorbing the emotions of other people, narcissists are only capable of sensing and feeling what they themselves feel. The feelings and thoughts of other people do not penetrate them.

These people could care less if you're sad or happy. They are only concerned with what they feel. Most of the time, that is pride and happiness for being who they are.

When you spend time with such people, never will you get the chance to talk about yourself. In the rare cases that you get to do so, the conversation is already over with them.

They have neither time nor interest to listen to other people talk about things that do not include them. But they think that everyone else has to know what they have been up to.

For an empath, that constitutes an unending demand for your attention and your appraisal. If you're not amazed by them, then you're not someone worth their time. Their constant demands will leave you with very little affection for yourself.

The Arrogant

In contrast to narcissists, arrogant people don't necessarily love themselves so much. In truth, they just think that they know better than anyone else.

Anything you say or do to them will always be interpreted as an upfront to how great they think themselves to be. No one is in a position to tell them anything, but they feel to be in a position to tell everyone what to do.

What they have is misplaced confidence. It may even be false confidence at times. Research has found that one of the biggest reasons behind arrogance is the reluctance to admit to insecurities.

You may have met someone like this at work, which is where these needs are born. Is there someone that thinks their work does not need correcting? How about that co-worker that refuses to take instruction and always insists on doing things their way? How about that colleague that snapped at you for pointing out a flaw in their work?

Whatever you do, you cannot reach them. Their minds are closed and will only accept praise and recognition from others. If you don't have that prepared for them, then you are a challenge to their capacities.

The Malicious

While arrogant and narcissistic people have high regards for themselves, they do not intentionally want to do anyone harm.

On the other hand, there are those people with the genuine intent of getting the better of you. These malicious minds are not focused on themselves, but would rather see you fail and stumble in order to satisfy themselves.

There are no cutting corners with these people. They want to hurt you and make you feel bad about yourself. This isn't because they have something against you. It's just because they enjoy seeing other people being miserable.

If they cannot get ahead of you or they cannot extort what they want from you, then they leave you alone. They are only interested in the people they can push around and bully.

The Jealous

For these people, they always think that they have the short end of the stick, even when things turn out in their favor. Everything is a poor comparison for them. You can give them the world on a plate but they'll still be able to point to someone who has something nicer.

They want what everyone else is enjoying. When they get that, they'll want something else. This makes it difficult for these people to become content with what they have. For them, blessings are consolation prizes meant to coddle their feelings of insecurity.

Being around these people will also teach you to belittle the blessings you have in your life. Instead of learning to celebrate the things you have accomplished, you'll be left feeling miserable as you think of all the irrelevant people you've never met, enjoying things you've never cared for.

The Down-Trodden

This could confuse you a little bit. Are the people you want to help the same people that you don't want in your life?

The problem with these kinds of people is that they are beyond help. You step in for them and help them once and you think you're done. The next moment, they're at your beck and call once more, asking for help.

You step in again and give your time and effort, hoping that their stream of misfortunes will end. Lo and behold, they're back again for more help.

You will initially reach out to them because, at the core, you need to help others will always stand out. You will understand their plights and empathize with them. You will then create an energy tie that will become a problem later on.

The more you help these people, the more they become dependent on you. For them, they are always the victim. Life is unfair and they are always the losers. Once something bad happens to them, they throw in the towel and resign themselves to their fate.

When you help them, they associate you with a merciful excuse not to help themselves. This continued dependence will drain and frustrate you at the same time. When it's too late, you realize you've become part of the problem by never giving them the chance to learn from their mistakes and grow on their own.

14 - Letting Go

Now that you know the kinds of toxicity that could be plaguing your life, do any people come into mind?

What about that co-worker that can't stop asking for favors? How about that boss that is never happy with your work? What about those in-laws that always seem to need something from you?

What about within your family? Are there people that constantly drain your energy and step over your boundaries? What do you do when their needs keep preceding yours?

The first thing you need to understand is the futility of meeting these people eye-to-eye.

Leveling with people of irrational behavior will only result in irrational results. These irrational results will only frustrate you. Forget about expending emotional energy trying to relate to these people. You will only end up just as miserable as they are.

Instead, accept the fact that these people will always be as they are and that can't be helped. The most you can do is to make sure that you don't end up like them. They're already a menace to the other people around them. Shall you bring the same influence into your own social circles?

An interesting thing about toxic people is that their behaviors become predictable once you identify them. Their erratic behaviors seem less destructive when you see them coming from a mile away. This gives you plenty of time to get out of their way or to prepare for their arrival.

Once you single them out from the other people in your life, it's easier to let go of the energy ties you have with this person. It's now easy for you to say that "you don't need any of that" and just walk away.

Another thing that becomes easier is understanding them. When you look at them for the damaged people that they are, you will find it in yourself to always be the bigger person and leave them to their devices.

On that note, it's always important that you be the bigger person. This is because you were born for that role when it comes to dealing with toxic people. You are destined to take the high road because you know that as the right thing to do. And the right thing is what always drives you.

Dealing With The Problem

What if you live with a toxic person? What if toxicity is in your family? What if you are married to a toxic person? What if walking away is not an option? Do you resign yourself to your fate and become another toxic person as well?

Naturally more difficult than just avoiding someone, tackling someone's toxicity requires a delicate approach.

The first thing that needs to be done is to let this toxic person know what they're doing to you. If this is someone close to you, then you should be as gentle and as understanding as possible.

Don't just say that they have a problem. Count back to times and instances where these people hurt you. Delineate how they made you feel and that you've already forgiven them for doing so.

At the same time, point out the fact that they have a problem that is putting a strain on your relationship. It is important not to be in a blaming position. For that, let them know that they are worth the trouble of helping.

If these people treasure whatever relationship they have with you, then reason will eventually find its way to them. As an empath, you will feel if what you're saying is getting to them. If the air around you gets lighter, then you'll know you're hitting a proper nerve and you're making progress.

If, on the unfortunate side, these people reject your pleas for adjustment and think you're on the offensive, take that as an indication that this person is completely beyond help. It will take something traumatic to get them to change – and that is something you want no part of.

In that case, it's alright to throw in the towel. You tried. You set your foot down. You brought things to their attention. If they don't want to work on improving your relationship with your help, then this person does not deserve your time and energy. It's time you started walking away, both in the physical and emotional sense.

15 - Conclusion

The lessons in this life manual will make it easier for you to manage your gifts as an empath. You may not have noticed it, but there is one underlying lesson beneath these techniques – loving yourself.

At your very core, you are a unique being that has been blessed with an extraordinary set of skills that make you a person among people. You are designed to get along with most people because you can immediately relate to them.

That is something you should treasure and protect with your very life. No matter what you do, preserving the quality of your life and the integrity of your talents should be your biggest priority.

Rejoice in the notion that loving yourself is not a crime. Your abilities rest on the cushion that is your emotional and mental health. If those are compromised, your gifts are as good as broken.

This is why you should ground yourself when you're overwhelmed.

This is why you should set and enforce boundaries when

you're dealing with others.

This is why you should learn to say no when it's against those boundaries.

This is why you should identify toxic people that are threats to your emotions.

This is why you should walk away from these people when working with them is no longer an option. Your happiness and well-being is not worth throwing away over a hopeless case.

Your next step from this book is to find another soul that needs the knowledge contained within this manual. As you were reading this, was there someone coming to mind?

Is there someone dear to you who is struggling with the people that surround them? Do you feel their pain whenever you're together? Perhaps it's time to let them know of their gifts and how to take care of them.

Thank you for reading!

Thank You

As we reach the end of this book, I want to say thanks for reading this book.

I want to get this information out to as many people as possible. If you found this book helpful, I would greatly appreciate you leaving me a review. This helps others find the book as well.

This book was self-published with the amazing help of Self-Publishing Made Easy Now! [3] . You can grab a free copy of the checklist that started my journey here: FREE Self-Publishing Checklist [4] .

[3]https://selfpublishingmadeeasynow.com/xpjv

[4]https://selfpublishingmadeeasynow.com/free_checklist

Disclaimer

This document is geared towards providing exact and reliable information in regards to the topic and issue covered. The publication is sold on the idea that the publisher is not required to render an accounting, officially permitted, or otherwise, qualified services. If advice is necessary, legal, financial, medical or professional, a practiced individual in the profession should be ordered.

This information is not presented by a financial or medical practitioner and is for entertainment, educational and informational purposes only. The content is not intended as a substitute for professional medical advice, diagnosis, or treatment. Always seek the advice of your physician or other qualified health care provider with any questions you may have regarding a medical condition. Never disregard professional medical advice or delay in seeking it because of something you have read.

The information provided herein is stated to be truthful and consistent, in that any liability, in terms of inattention or otherwise, by any usage or abuse of any policies, processes, or directions contained within is the solitary and utter responsibility of the recipient reader. Under no circumstances will any legal responsibility or blame be held against the publisher for any reparation, damages, or monetary loss due to the information herein, either directly or indirectly.

www.ingramcontent.com/pod-product-compliance
Ingram Content Group UK Ltd.
Pitfield, Milton Keynes, MK11 3LW, UK
UKHW021909190726
13853UKWH00002B/587